"Jennifer Bird has written an accessible, encouraging, and enlightening guide to understanding the Bible better. For those who love the Bible but have serious questions about it, *Permission Granted* offers information, fellowship, and ultimately the freedom to learn and explore without fear. This is a winsome yet challenging read that made me love the Bible all the more."

—RACHEL HELD EVANS, author of *A Year of Biblical Womanhood* and *Searching for Sunday*

"*Permission Granted* is an excellent reentry point for honest, adult engagement with the Bible, whether you have been touched by it or burned by it (or both). This book is passionate without sacrificing compassion, academically informed but accessible. Jennifer Bird's voice is a unique and important one: warm and witty, sage and occasionally snarky, but ultimately deeply reflective and profoundly serious about the troubles many people have with the Bible and how it is used by people today."

—JOSEPH A. MARCHAL, Associate Professor of Religious Studies, Ball State University

"Jennifer G. Bird is one of those professional readers of the Bible, and they are few and far between, who can both approach the texts as a sophisticated academic critic and translate such research and reading for everyday readers in lucid and effective fashion. Her goal throughout *Permission Granted—Take the Bible into Your Own Hands* is to get readers to read and to think on their own, drawing on their lives and experiences, as they go through difficult themes and texts. This she does with wisdom and power, with respect and kindness. I recommend the volume most heartily."

—FERNANDO F. SEGOVIA, Oberlin Graduate Professor of New Testament and Early Christianity, Vanderbilt University

"Jennifer Bird is a God-wrestler who is willing to talk back to the Bible when it doesn't make sense. Though some might be offended by her claims, I consider Bird's book to be an excellent model for authentic discipleship and adult faith, written in very accessible, easy-flowing language."

—MORGAN GUYTON, Director, NOLA Wesley Campus Ministry and Blogger at Patheos.com

"In a distinctly personal style, Jennifer Bird invites us to honor our own questions about the Bible. Rather than submit to scripture because 'we're supposed to' or rejecting the Bible as irrelevant, Bird supplies readers with fresh information and new perspectives for making their own judgments on issues ranging from biblical sexualities and violence to what it means to believe in Jesus."

—GREG CAREY, Professor of New Testament,
Lancaster Theological Seminary

"Curious about the Bible? Jennifer Bird's *Permission Granted—Take the Bible into Your Own Hands* gives you the tools to explore the Bible on your own. It provides clear questions and specific examples to help you reach your own conclusions about what the Bible means for you."

—NYASHA JUNIOR, Assistant Professor of Hebrew Bible/Old
Testament, Howard University School of Divinity

"A great many academic biblical scholars, trained to read the Bible critically, previously read the Bible literally. Jennifer Grace Bird is one such scholar, but unlike most scholars she is able to write about the Bible in ways that nonacademic Bible readers will find accessible, engaging, and enlightening. This is not the only book of its kind, but, to my mind, it is the best of its kind. Unusual for a work of biblical scholarship, it has the potential to transform nonacademic lives."

—STEPHEN D. MOORE, Edmund S. Janes Professor of New
Testament Studies, The Theological School, Drew University

"Jennifer Bird has the rare skill of being able to write with flair for a nonacademic audience. Her impressive learning as a biblical scholar and her range of changing experiences in confessional and nonconfessional contexts are used to help guide the reader carefully and sensitively through some of the biggest topics in popular understandings of the Bible. Rather than simply dictate answers, Bird opens up opportunities for the reader to engage with the texts and the issues for themselves. I would warmly recommend this excellent book to anyone beginning the study of the Bible and to those who wish to explore alternatives to received understandings."

—JAMES CROSSLEY, Professor of Bible, Culture and Politics,
University of Sheffield, UK

Permission Granted

Permission Granted

Take the Bible into Your Own Hands

Jennifer Grace Bird

WESTMINSTER
JOHN KNOX PRESS
LOUISVILLE · KENTUCKY

Book design by Drew Stevens
Cover design by Dilu Nicholas

Library of Congress Cataloging-in-Publication Data

Bird, Jennifer G.
  Permission granted : take the Bible into your own hands / Jennifer Grace Bird. -- First edition.
    pages cm
  ISBN 978-0-664-26040-8 (alk. paper)
  1. Bible--Criticism, interpretation, etc. I. Title.
  BS511.3.B625 2015
  220.6--dc23
                                                                          2014035970

Most Westminster John Knox Press books are available at special quantity discounts when purchased in bulk by corporations, organizations, and special-interest groups. For more information, please e-mail SpecialSales@wjkbooks.com.

*For Marianne and Jennings Bird,
my parents, my cheerleaders, my heroes*

Contents

Acknowledgments   ix
Introduction   xi

1. What the Bible Is and Is Not   1
2. Two Creation Stories and Other Myths   13
3. What Really Happened in the Garden?   25
4. Sex: Who, What, and Why?   35
5. Violence: The Language Everyone Understands   55
6. Cover-Ups and Edited Stories   75
7. Biblical Women: Silent, Submissive Baby Makers?   95
8. Born of a Virgin?   121
9. Will the Real Jesus Please Stand Up?   131
10. Was Paul the First Christian?   155
11. Judgment Day Is . . . Not Coming   167
12. Now What?   187

Acknowledgments

I must first thank my editor, Jessica Miller Kelley, whose revisionary flair never once detracted from my own voice and who was a delight to work with every step of the way. Thank you, thank you. Thank you to Bridgett Green, biblical studies acquisitions editor for WJK, for seeing us as a good fit, and to the decision makers who gave this manuscript a chance.

I would like to thank the friends and family who read over early, and often way-too-long, versions of this project: Mark Exline, Joey Frenette, Teri Hammer, Leah Holle, Ty Jesse, Jessica Johnson, Roberta Lewis, Jessie Lindley-Curtice, Amanda Maness, Lori Matweeff, Ben McCarthy, Maureen Olsen, Aaron O'Neal, Paul Raker, Christine Vargas, and anyone else I have unintentionally overlooked. Most especially Brian Hughes, Pam Israel, and Whitney Keller, who all held up a flag of concern regarding the tone in early versions, which sent me back into a kind conversational mode, time and again. Brian's unflagging excitement for and input on this project, which gave me a boost too many times to count, cannot be adequately acknowledged, so I hope this nod will suffice.

I could not have done the writing of this manuscript in such a focused way had it not been for the emotional and financial support of my parents; brother, Patrick; and sister-in-law, Lise Rowe; and for Bridget Saladino's generosity of spirit and space, as she opened her home to me for the year of this project.

I'd like to thank Susan Sassmann and Kenny Shulman for telling me to get on with it. I'm ever so grateful to Jessica Bailey for the title, and to Jessica, Donna Deviney, Caye Spain, and Cindy Robbins for their moral support and general mother-like pride in what I am doing. To the two focus groups of rowdy, bawdy women who gathered with me to offer early input on the direction of this project: I am so grateful for those evenings and your ongoing excitement and support. My regular hikes and conversations with my Aunt Pam kept me grounded in the midst of this tumultuous, however exciting, journey.

The family and friends who made my summer promotional tour possible—Marianne and Jennings Bird, Kathryn Freeman, Teri Hammer, Abigail Henrich Sydnor, Brian and Jenevieve Hughes, Ellin and Al Jimmerson, Lynn and Barry Seaton, and Peterson Toscano and Glen Retief — gave me the gifts of warm and generous hospitality, thoughtful connections in their communities, a larger vision for how to employ this project, and, indirectly, last-minute revisionary nuggets for the manuscript. Bridget Saladino, Shane Shine, and Katie Bennett at Bridge Advantage made the marketing end of that trip possible. I am gratefully indebted to this august group for it all.

Finally, I am grateful to all the students I taught in introductory courses while in North Carolina, at Greensboro College, Guilford College, Rockingham Community College, and UNC-Greensboro. They are the people who helped me to refine my approach to these conversations. It is my hope that this book offers its readers similar moments of laughter, shock, disorientation, and freedom that regularly transpired within those classrooms.

Introduction

One of the main reasons people of faith read the Bible is to find out who God is and how we as humans can expect to relate to this God. The Bible, from this perspective, is a source of encouragement and faith formation. It is, for many people, a reminder that God is love and is in control, and that God wants good things for us, ultimately. Many people also see the Bible as a resource to turn to for knowing how to live one's life so that one's relationship with God will be a rich and meaningful one.

That is why I used to put a great deal of time into memorizing passages: I would then have God's words of insight and guidance with me at all times, and I could think and speak using God's words. This is why so many people have daily Bible readings in the morning or devote a portion of their daily schedule to personal Bible study. It is similar to investing in a relationship: if someone wants to know and love God or Jesus well, then they will put time into that relationship in a disciplined way. Even if this is not your reality, I hope you can see why so many people see it this way.

All these motivations were at work in my life. My relationship with Jesus was the most important thing in my life, to the point where I went on dates with Jesus, from time to time, in college. Yes, you read that correctly—I dated Jesus in college. I was not the only person I knew doing this, for it was seen as a form of piety, by many of my friends, at the time. "We" did things like go out for breakfast or to my favorite donut shop. It was time dedicated to, well, contemplating Jesus and life's mysteries. Reading and understanding what the Bible said was of ultimate importance for me.

For years I had many people telling me what the Bible said or meant, which was often quite enriching for me. There were times when people would turn to the Hebrew or the Greek in order to prove a point, which always seemed to hold more sway for me than simply relying on the English translation. It did not matter if I did not like what they said; it was, to me, a more honest handling of the Bible, thus it was a message I was more inclined to listen to. The closer to the original source, the more pure the message seemed to me to be. Perhaps you can see why the original languages had primacy for me and why my interest in them took me to seminary.

Two of the most influential women in my life, in my college and post-college years, were either already ordained or were seeking ordination. My mother was the one already ordained. On the day of her ordination—a day second in importance only to giving birth to her children—I had been so bold as to let her know what I knew scripture said about women's ordination: I said that I did not understand how she could do such a thing, since it is against God's Word. What's fascinating about this is that I had grown up in a church that regularly had female pastors, all of whom I had loved and appreciated at the time. The fact that I could swing so far in my view of the ordination of women is a testament to how deeply the content of the Bible came to hold truth for me, over and against what others said or did.

To her credit, my mom did not push me out of the van as we were flying down the highway. Instead, she told me her story, the story of her journey that had brought her to the place of seeking ordination. Though I had seen this story play out, I had never known her side of its development. I was struck by what a conundrum this all was for me. The way she told it, it was never a matter of her wanting the role of pastor. Rather, the hand of God had guided her experience through members of our church appreciating and needing her to use her gifts.

In short, her experience had trumped the way I was reading the Bible, my final rule or authority. For me, experience was to be interpreted or directed in light of what the Bible said; it was never to be the other way around. This was one of the few times in my life that I have been speechless. I could not argue with what she had experienced even though her experience clashed with my convictions. Oy vey!

The next few years after her ordination, I continued to live my life with great enthusiasm for the commands and guidelines I saw within the scriptures. At times this meant wearing (newly purchased) baggy clothing for the sake of not causing my boyfriend to stumble. At other times, it meant finding ways to make sense of and be okay with difficult passages. Just because I did not like something in scripture did not mean I could disregard it. It was all God's Word. Thus, there remained some form of tension or confusion for me, most intensely regarding the ordination of women.

There came a day when someone handed me a forty-page paper on women in leadership in the church. At the time I was told that, given my gifts in leadership and ministry, I could go as high as I wanted to in the para-church organization I was working in, even be president. But I just couldn't be the main pastor in a church. The paper justified this position, and it was what I also believed at the time. Primarily, women were not permitted to be in ultimate authority over a church or men in general (1 Tim. 2:11), but they could use their gifts, if done appropriately (1 Cor. 12, Rom. 12). The thesis was backed by other biblical passages, most importantly parts of Genesis 2–3, the place where all things began, if you will.

Shortly thereafter, I received a copy of a master's thesis in the mail, written by another important woman in my life. She focused on the "Martha and Mary" passage (Luke 10:38–42). The day I received her thesis, I immediately sat on the stairs leading up to my bedroom and read it, cover to cover. In it, this friend did something that shook me to my core. Working with the Greek text, she took the story to be saying that Jesus was affirming Mary, not just for sitting at his feet, but for choosing for herself. In this thesis, my friend had referenced me, by name, as an example of a Martha, giving in to what others expected of me. She had watched me not make my own choices, to my own detriment.

It was not just that my friend was saying that she believed in me that moved me. It was that someone, motivated by a passionate faith and a desire to be a follower of Christ, had seen something in the Bible that said that women could be true to themselves, and it was Jesus himself saying it! If someone could see this kind of a shift in the meaning of that passage, by looking at the nuances in the Greek, what other passages were up for such reconsideration?

That, my friends, is what ultimately had me moving cross-country to begin the three year Master of Divinity degree at Princeton Theological Seminary. I went to learn languages, and I learned them well. I went because my love of Jesus and for studying God's word were the most important things in my life. And if I was going to be taking my cues in life from this book, and such subtle nuances could exist in it, then I wanted to be able to study those terms and their nuances for myself.

People often say that the first year of seminary shakes a person's foundation, the second stirs up what is left, and the third is a year of rebuilding. I lived this pattern to a T. I was challenged to see the Bible and my theological convictions in new ways that first year, to the point where, at times, it felt like a crisis of faith.

There are two things that allowed me to keep my head above water. The first was the assurance that God had given me my mind, thus it had to be okay to apply it to my faith (some people refer to this as "faith seeking understanding"). The second was the realization that if I could not at least consider new ideas about God and the Bible, if they could not handle being prodded and questioned, then they were not really worth my devotion. I concluded that both God and the Bible could handle my intellectual pursuits. In fact, it seemed to me then and still does to this day that it is the ultimate statement of respect for God to take ideas about God and the Bible so seriously.

So, while I am not trying to offer to a reader everything that I gained in seminary, or the subsequent years of PhD work, it is my intention to touch on the most salient points about the Bible that I have benefitted from learning and thinking about. These are also what I have found to be some of the juiciest topics for people, based on the dozens of Introduction to the Bible classes that I have taught. My two main goals are to invite you to engage your curiosity while reading passages from the Bible and to consider the issues I raise as they relate to the Bible. Let all these things inform your thinking as you take the Bible into your own hands.

For people of faith, these conversations sometimes initially involve a mixture of shock and uncertainty. The shock is usually due to never having heard the full story before, and wondering why they hadn't! The uncertainty is usually due to being uncomfortable with the implications of this new information. For those of you feeling uncertain and uncomfortable, I would remind you of the two assurances that kept me afloat:

1. God gave you your brain, so it has to be okay to use it.
2. If they are worth your devotion, God and the Bible can handle your intellectual pursuits.

For those who are not so deeply connected to the Bible, who have perhaps pieced together an impression of scripture from popular culture and the loudest voices on the metaphorical street corner, the invitation still applies. Instead of leaning on what you have always heard about the Bible, you are now invited to read and consider it for yourself. The conversations we had in my introductory courses were so important and refreshing that it seemed to me that they ought to be happening in places beyond college classrooms and campuses. This is my attempt to invite you—no matter what your age, religious background, or academic experience—into similar conversations and thoughtful engagement with the Bible.

The title of this book, *Permission Granted*, comes from watching the faces of faithful, smart students go from looking concerned to relieved as I told them that it is okay to think about these things for themselves. It was as if they had been waiting for years for the "go ahead" to apply their minds to what they saw on the pages of the Bible! But I understood why they were hesitant and that it came, primarily, from their respect for the Bible and the people who had taught them about it for years.

You will find that I begin every new topic by asking you to take stock of your own thoughts and beliefs related to the topic at hand. To this end, I also often pose a few questions to help draw out your thoughts on the topic. It helps to be clear about where you are starting, in any conversation. You might even find it helpful to discuss these things with a friend or partner.

I will also ask you to pause and think about things, from time to time. So much of what is contained in this book is simply me pointing out what is there, or what is conspicuously not in there, so reading the scriptures for yourself is essential. (If you don't have a Bible handy, www.biblegateway.com is good.) In short, I urge you to read this book actively, not passively. Passive reading is what happens when you find yourself at the bottom of a page and realize you have no idea what it said. Active reading requires that you envision the stories as you read, engage your curiosity about the stories, and think through the implications of it all. Active reading requires a certain amount of critical (reflective) thought. You do not have to agree with what I say, but I encourage you to at least give the ideas a chance. Otherwise, this book will not be nearly as interesting or productive as it could be for you.

This leads me to a quotation, attributed to Aristotle, which summarizes a great deal of what this book is about: "It is the mark of an educated mind to entertain a thought without accepting it." Notice the depth of familiarity implied in "entertaining a thought," such as when we entertain guests at our homes. We invite them in, make them feel welcome and comfortable. Above all, we are seeking to know and understand our guests, whether or not we come to agree with every position they hold or become close friends. This is what it looks like to entertain a thought. You do not have to agree with something in order to understand it. But I don't think it is fair to dismiss something you have not yet tried diligently to understand.

Part of the point of this book is to make some scholarly material more readily accessible to a general public than it tends to be, and thus I will do my best to explain, in context, what may be new concepts for some readers. Also, as you read through this book, you will see that there is a good deal of "see also chapter ___" parenthetical comments. This is not meant to be purely self-referential; rather it is highlighting the complexity of scripture and that any one topic can be approached from multiple angles.

If you are the type of person to read only the chapters that most interest you, I understand but nonetheless encourage you, even plead with you, to read chapter 1 first. There are some significant ideas and points in that chapter that carry over into all the others.

Finally, let me reassure you that I am not trying to "poke holes" in anyone's faith. I am trying to help you see the nature of some of the passages in the Bible in a way that respects it, even if it is a startlingly new perspective. Seeing any part of the Bible differently than you did before does not change who God is, it simply changes the way you see how the Bible helps you relate to God. For those who have knee-jerk reactions to challenging what they have always thought or been told about the Bible, let me be the one to assure you that it is understandable to respond that way and then to encourage you to go ahead, take the Bible into your own hands, and consider all these things for yourself.

Permission granted.

1
What the Bible Is and Is Not

As we begin the discussion about what the Bible is and is not, take a few moments to take stock of your own view of the Bible. Is it a source of inspiration? Is it the mouthpiece of God, through which you and your faith community hear what God has to say to you? Is it something you read for daily devotion?

Similarly, take a moment to think about the nature of the Bible. Reflect on the words that you choose to use to describe it and what they mean. For instance, if you say every word is inspired by God, do you mean that the Bible is inerrant and infallible? Or was it inspired in a more general sense, in that the wisdom it contains was written by people greatly inspired?

Have you ever seen the bumper sticker that says, "God said it. I believe it. That settles it."? Of course, while I am sure not everyone reading this book will think of the Bible in this way, I do think it is helpful to understand where someone who does is coming from. Grasping why some people believe with all their being that the Bible is inerrant and infallible can be quite enlightening.

Let's begin with that word *inerrant*. *Inerrant* simply means "free from error." Using this word to describe the Bible is usually a way to say something about its trustworthiness. A person who uses this word typically believes that God inspired absolutely everything within the Bible. Thus, every word on every page, every promise and command is intended and relevant for the believer reading it today. The level of

What's in a Name?

The names that I am using to refer to the two testaments in the Christian Bible might be new to you. I would like to explain what they mean and why I make this choice.

If you approach the Bible from a Christian perspective, you will most likely think of it as having two testaments: the Old and the New. (You might also think of it as including the Apocrypha, but that is another matter.) The thing is, the books in the "Old Testament" make up the entire Bible for Jews. Thus it is a bit disrespectful to refer to the primary set of Jewish sacred writings with a label that implies that something newer and better has come along. So, out of respect for the fact that Christians and Jews both read that first testament, I prefer not to call it the "Old Testament."

But finding a way to refer to that testament respectfully gets a bit tricky. The Jewish Bible and the Christian Old Testament use all the same books, but in different orders. The Jewish Bible groups and orders them by genre: the Torah (first five books), the Prophets, and the Writings. Using the first letter of the Hebrew words for each section, we get the acronym T.N.K., pronounced Tanak. But since the Tanak and the Old Testament have a slightly different ordering of the books, they tell different overall stories. From this perspective, then, they are not exactly the same thing.

Some people make the suggestion that the two testaments be referred to as the First and the Second Testaments. I like that this suggestion honors the historical development, without implying that the Christian tradition has replaced Judaism.

Finally, some suggest that we call it the "Hebrew Bible" as a way to refer to the language it was written in, originally (although a small portion was written in Aramaic).

I hope that you can begin to see how complicated this matter is! For ease or convenience, I prefer to call it the "Hebrew Bible."

When it comes to the New Testament we still have a bit of a labeling issue. If I had gone with "First Testament" for the Hebrew Bible, we could call this the Second Testament. But I did not in this case. Similarly, some people suggest calling it the Newer Testament, or the Christian Testament. Now, this last one is not entirely accurate, since both testaments in the Christian Bible are "Christian," strictly speaking. All these concerns noted, I will refer to the New Testament as the "Newer Testament."

If you are wondering why some people make such a big deal out of labels or names, consider how powerful our words and language are. Think about the time people put into choosing names for their children. Even nicknames that we give to one another matter and have meaning. The adage "Sticks and stones may break my bones, but words will never hurt me" is not entirely true. Ask anyone who has been verbally bullied. Words can wound. Words can also give life. Our language and the ways we choose to talk about something do have power and do matter to us.

This is why I am careful about how I refer to the contents of Bible, which has been cherished by millions of people around the world, over many centuries. I hope you will join me in being similarly thoughtful about the way you choose to talk about it.

One final caveat on names and labels: The first time I heard someone call the scriptures "writings" or even, brace yourself, "texts," I was so shocked I didn't hear another word of that lecture. How dare he be so casual with the Bible! However, there is nothing wrong with calling the books of the Bible "texts" or "writings," since that is precisely what they are. When I use these labels, I do not mean to offend, and I assure you that I take these scriptures quite seriously.

trust in this way of thinking is difficult to describe adequately; you trust God, so you trust that God carefully directed how the Bible was made, at every step along the way.

This perspective usually goes hand-in-hand with the idea that the Bible is as perfect as God is perfect. If you pause to consider the implications of this belief, the stakes are quite high for a person defending the Bible's inerrancy. Saying the Bible isn't perfect may feel tantamount to challenging who God is, and if you are going to question that, where does the questioning stop? It feels like an all-or-nothing gig.

This is how I saw things at one point, so I can empathize with this conviction. The first time someone I respected challenged the Bible's inerrancy, this thing called a "slippery slope" suddenly became very real to me. As you can imagine, that level of questioning does not appeal to a person who believes that "all scripture is God-breathed and is useful for teaching, rebuking, correcting, and training in righteousness" (1 Tim. 3:16). This verse is, after all, a significant part of why so many Christians take this inerrancy approach to the Bible. Scripture being "God-breathed" is also taken to mean that it is "God-inspired." The reference to "all scripture" is taken to mean everything contained in the

Christian Bible. The reasons are mounting for why some people get defensive when someone suggests that there are errors or contradictions within the Bible.

So, in light of these things, I invite you to take a few moments to mull over the following two points:

1. WHAT SCRIPTURE DOES 1 TIMOTHY 3:16 REFER TO?

The letter of 1 Timothy was written before the Gospels and letters that make up the Newer Testament were considered to be "scripture." The author of 1 Timothy would have been writing from the tradition of Judaism. So "scripture" referred only to the passages in the Torah, Prophets, and Writings that he would have been familiar with.

Additionally, the author of 1 Timothy could not have anticipated the formation of the Newer Testament (which was formalized in the late fourth century), much less that his letter would be included in it. Some people (including myself, at one time) might claim that God knew what writings would eventually be considered scripture, wanted this line to refer to all scripture, and therefore inspired 1 Timothy's author to say those things. Viewing the Bible as inerrant makes such reasoning possible, but it doesn't take seriously the writer's actual context or intention.

Perhaps the most important aspect of this question that I hope you will think about is this: if you have a passage in scripture that says that all scripture is God-breathed, then you have a self-validating system or an example of "circular reasoning." Think about this for a moment. While convenient, I do not think that God would endorse such sneakiness.

2. WHAT DID "GOD-BREATHED" MEAN?

Now that we know that *scripture* meant the Hebrew Bible, we are still left with a conundrum: how are we to understand the "God-breathed" part? Would the original recipients have thought it meant that every word in the Hebrew Bible was as God intended, as many people take it to mean today? Or would they have thought of it in the generally inspired kind of way? Would the original audience have thought that it meant that there would be no errors, in terms of names and places and dates, and that every story happened just as it is narrated, as many people do today? Of course, we will never know. But here are a few insights for you to consider, for now. We will get into more depth on these topics throughout the book.

Let's take the idea that all the stories in the Bible happened exactly as they are told to us. This is, for instance, what people believe to be the case when they hold to a strict Creationist perspective on the origins of the planet. They read the first couple of chapters of Genesis as a narration of what transpired "in the beginning." Aside from this being a bit difficult, since no one was there to transcribe what God said and did, there are logical problems to the poetic order described in Genesis 1, such as the occurrence of day and night before there was a sun to rise and set.

As for the matter of there being no inaccuracies, in terms of names or dates or places, you could compare Judges 1 with Joshua 10. Joshua's narrative makes it clear that the Israelites kill everyone they come across, slaughtering town after town full of people. Judges tells us that the Israelites did not drive out the inhabitants of the land but that the Canaanites remained and the Israelites settled among them. Surely these cannot both have transpired. But there is a way to read both accounts that respects them and does not require that you ditch your faith as a result. It does require that you read with an understanding of the stories' contexts and why they were written and at least a dose of how histories were told and passed down at the time.

On the matter of every word being exactly as God intended it to be, consider juxtaposing the following passages. Exodus 34:6: "The LORD, the LORD, a God merciful and gracious, slow to anger, and abounding in steadfast love and faithfulness." Compare this with Genesis 6:6, where God is said to regret having made humankind, or Exodus 32:9-10, where God calls the Israelites "stiff-necked" people and wants to let the divine wrath consume them. Can those all be accurate representations of God? Maybe we can read some of these passages in a way that honors them, without having to attribute them all to God's intention. But if they are all read literally, then there seems to be a contradiction in there, somewhere.

What about what we see in scripture regarding murder? The sixth commandment, of the "Top 10," says not to murder, clear and simple. Yet, the LORD also tells the Israelites to slaughter towns full of people and to put people to death as a consequence for many offenses described in the other commandments. So, which is it?

While the idea that the Bible is God-inspired can be quite a comforting thought, taking this idea literally can set people up to expect the Bible to be a kind of book that it is not, leading to some very

uncomfortable mental gymnastics in the attempt to reconcile conflicting statements and one's own experience.

The Bible is actually a collection of writings. The books of the Bible
were all written by humans. They did not descend from the heavens as
one perfect whole, bound together, Genesis to Revelation. Many of the
books of the Hebrew Bible were written down hundreds of years after
the events they narrate. Think about how the stories would have been
adapted over time, for different audiences and situations. We see something similar with some of the Newer Testament writings, primarily with
the Gospels and Acts. The earliest Gospel was written down at least thirty
years after Jesus' execution and resurrection, and the latest was another
thirty years later. The book of Acts depicts what Jesus' disciples did in the
early 30s but was not committed to writing until the mid-80s.

Perhaps it is okay, then, to begin to rethink how you see the writings
in the Bible. The idea of scripture being perfect, as many people would
have us believe, needs to be set aside. Did those authors believe that
they were capturing events exactly as they had happened? Is that even
possible or a reasonable thing to suggest?

Some people would counter that God told them exactly what to
write and that is how the authors were able to write without errors. I see
the appeal of this belief, since I used to hold it myself. But somewhere
in the process of the writing of these texts, this belief becomes difficult
to uphold. Was it the original version (none of which we still have)
that was inspired? For many of the scriptures, what we have today are
copies of copies that include small, and sometimes significant, add-ons.
Furthermore, though we turn to the same basic collection of hundreds
of manuscripts (in ancient Hebrew, Aramaic, and Greek) to produce a
copy of the Bible today, we know that a saying in any language will lose
something in translation to our modern languages. So which version is
exactly what God wanted?

The books of the Bible were written for various reasons, employing
several genres. Most, if not all, of the Bible was written by men and
from their perspectives. So, let's take a look at why motivations, genres,
and perspective matter.

MOTIVATION BEHIND THE WRITINGS

I have heard many people say that the Bible is best understood as: Basic
Instructions Before Leaving Earth—B.I.B.L.E. This approach to the

Bible says that we can read the words on the pages as they present themselves, trusting that God's truths are eternal and that God's Spirit will reveal to you the truths you need to hear. But if you have not stopped to ask what it was that people thought they were communicating to others when they told the first story of creation in Genesis 1 (see chap. 2), or why someone was writing down David's story at all (chap. 6), or even what we should expect from a biography of Jesus (chap. 9), then there is a good chance we will look for and expect to find the wrong things in the words of the Bible.

Whatever the original motivations at work were, we do know that they were written to inspire faith in God and to give the original faith community a sense of collective identity. No question. But that does not mean that we should expect all the stories to have taken place just as they are told. In fact, in some cases, it does not even matter if the stories took place at all. What matters is that the stories are there and have defined reality and identities for millions of people over the centuries. They have even inspired countless masterpieces, without which our world would be much the poorer.

But there are also stories and passages in the Bible that seem to have been written to justify some pretty horrific things. Thus, as reasonable, rational, and loving people, we might want to be able to say that some parts of the Bible are not inspired by God but by humans (chaps. 5 and 7).

It is also worth noting that the purpose and the genre—why someone writes and the form he wrote in—are often intimately connected. This leads us to the discussion of genres found in the Bible.

GENRES IN THE BIBLE

Being aware of the different genres used in the Bible allows you to read a passage appropriately. There are many people who believe that the truth contained in the Bible is entirely self-evident, such that one can find a line anywhere within the Bible and immediately apply it to one's life. Similarly, one can connect two lines or passages, if they have a word or idea in common, and they can serve to support each other, regardless of the context of each passage. This practice is often called "cherry-picking," because people pick and choose which verses to read and leave others out. In pairing passages based on shared ideas, however, we often overlook the all-important context and form of the writing.

The list of genres used in the Bible might surprise you. Histories are the most common type of story. A good deal of the Hebrew Bible is comprised of this genre, but it is also found in Acts in the Newer Testament. There are also songs and hymns, especially the one hundred fifty contained in Psalms, though they are also strewn throughout the Bible in various places. There is poetry, even love poetry between two lovers not yet living in the same home, in the Song of Solomon. The Gospels are most akin to ancient biographies, which are different from modern biographies. There are personal letters and letters written to communities. There is political propaganda. (Yikes! That's a scary one!) There is even politically subversive writing in the Bible. The writing contained in the books of the Prophets is its own kind of a genre, appropriately labeled "prophetic literature." There are a couple instances of apocalyptic literature, as well: parts of Daniel and the entire book of Revelation.

Perhaps most unsettling for those hearing it the first time is that there are also myths in the Bible. When I say *myth*, I mean this in the proper sense of the word, not in the "that's nothing but a lie" connotation (see chap. 2). *Myths* are stories that were written to explain something unexplainable at the time, such as a natural phenomenon (a rainbow); to give a backstory that explains certain cultural practices (Israelites' weekly day of rest); or to give a "reason" for things such as women's severe pain in childbirth.

The fact that stories were written for particular reasons does not change what is in them. But it might change the way you think about the stories. Most often when people begin to read with context and writing type in mind, they find the writings more meaningful, not less.

VOICE OF THE AUTHORS

When I talk about the voice of the authors, I am referring to two things about the biblical content: from whose perspective the stories are told and whose concerns are represented.

First, not only were the books of the Bible written by humans, and not dictated directly by God, but they were also almost exclusively written by men. In other words, we get very little in the Bible from the perspective of women. Even the stories written about women, or that have women protagonists, are likely written by men. Please pause to consider the implications of this fact. Sometimes people get uncomfortable or slightly defensive when they first consider this issue. Many of my students have responded to hearing this by wondering if I hate men. My opinion of the males among us is not the issue, though. This aspect of the Bible, the sex of its authors, has far-reaching implications. Let's look at why that is the case.

I do not wish to start some sort of battle of the sexes here, nor do I wish to overgeneralize about men or women. But for a moment, think about the people in your life, both male and female (and any who fall somewhere in between). Do you have a sense of how a group of men sitting around a campfire might tell stories as compared to how a group of women might do the same? Then consider that we have hundreds of stories, all told from the perspective of men. In lacking women's voices and perspectives, we are also missing what matters to them in these stories. If we take into consideration how patriarchal the culture was that produced the Bible—by *patriarchal* I mean a culture in which males are the head of each family and dominant in every regard—then we can be safe in assuming that patriarchal values will play out in the stories as we find them.

Many people would suggest that we not judge these ancient cultures based on our modern values. I agree. This is not meant to be a judgment on people from a different time and place. This is merely an observation that I think is crucial for you to consider in terms of what you will find in the scriptures. After all, though some of our cultural values have changed, we continue to turn to scriptures with ancient patriarchal value systems. Take a moment to think about this tension.

Additionally, what this means is that it can be rather enlightening to stop and try to think through any given story from the perspective of a woman who is in it, regardless of whether or not she is named or has any lines. It can be a rather fun exercise, if you are up for it.

For instance, why not think through the story of Noah from the perspective of his wife? (Your version of her might be slightly different than Jennifer Connelly's character in the 2014 blockbuster.) Can you imagine what questions she might ask Noah? What about when Abraham and Sarah pretend that they are siblings so that the Egyptians would not kill Abraham and take Sarah for themselves (Gen. 12)? Ever wonder what that first night was like for her, as the newest addition to Pharaoh's harem? Or perhaps sort through a bigger story, such as Abraham's almost-sacrifice of Isaac from Sarah's perspective. She was not consulted by Abraham in this matter; he simply took their son and went for a three-day hike. Hmmmm. That would not go over very well with any of the mothers that I know today.

We could look at a story in John 8, which is typically called, "The Woman Caught in Adultery." Even this label raises questions, since the last time I checked it took two to tango. (Where is the man?) If you read that story from her perspective, instead of focusing on what Jesus does, you might be surprised by the questions that come to mind. Many of my students have suggested it be called "The Woman Framed for Adultery" or "Jesus Calls Out Hypocrisy." They might not be as catchy, but they highlight a very different aspect of that story than when you label it focusing on the woman's sexual behavior. My point here is that not only are the stories quite rich with possibilities, in terms of how to read them, but even the way our Bibles label stories has an influence on how we read and on what we expect of the people in the stories.

What about Separation of Church and State?

Whenever I talk about how the Bible has an influence on people's political and social choices, someone always protests that there should be a separation of church and state. Keep in mind that "Separation of Church and State" was intended to protect our religious and worship choices and practices. It was not about protecting the State from your faith. Your beliefs and religious convictions go with you everywhere and inform everything you do. It does not make sense for them to be separated from what you do in the realms of politics and society.

I know many people who think of themselves as faithful Christians who will state that they are not concerned about politics. Their focus is on the spiritual aspect of their faith, which makes sense given all the time and energy put into talking about a person's personal "walk" or "spiritual growth." While these are all great things, the focus on the individual tends to take our attention off of the social realm that we all share.

To deny that our beliefs and convictions do affect how we behave politically is to deny that we live in communities together. Since we clearly live in communities together, we are political people (the Greek term for "city" is *polis*). If you draw your worldview primarily from scripture, you are perpetuating some of those ancient values, not just within your homes but in society as well, often without even realizing it. This is, indeed, something to think about.

Perhaps you are starting to see what I mean by raising the issue of who is telling the stories. You might want to be conscious of who seems to be narrating these stories. If the narrator tends to take a man's perspective, what are we missing? It also means that the stories will reflect the cultural expectations of men and women at that time.

Second, in terms of why voice matters, pay attention to what the stories indicate are the matters of concern. For instance, what kinds of assumptions about who God is does the author build on? What message does a story send about how we can treat one another? Since these stories are in the Bible, many people assume that their messages are de facto acceptable. But just because we see something in the Bible does not mean that it is something we should be perpetuating today. (If you need some specific examples to back up this last claim, chaps. 4, 5, and 7 are good ones to turn to next.)

CONCLUSION

The human authorship of the books is important to keep in mind, as is an awareness of genre, as you read the Bible. On some level, this can actually be reassuring. It means that mistakes or duplicate stories with very different messages do not need to cause a crisis of faith. It also means that there might be messages that you think no longer apply, and you can embrace this realization instead of ignore it.

I cannot recall how many people have asked me why I ask so many questions about the Bible instead of "just believing what it says." I understand that they were simply getting tired of my challenging what they had always believed. But it also concerns me when an adult believes that she cannot ask questions, whether it is of her partner or spouse, her pastor, or the book she turns to for guidance in life—the Bible. If we cannot ask questions of these sources of guidance and direction, or of our life companions, why are we trusting them to such a deeply personal degree? Similarly, if you believe that God created you with the mind that you have, why would God say that you can apply your mind to everything in this world except for how you read the Bible? So allow me to be the one to say it: You are free to apply your brilliant mind to matters even as important as your faith and your understanding of the Bible!

Permission granted.

 TAKE THE BIBLE INTO YOUR OWN HANDS

1. What terms do you prefer to use for the two testaments of the Bible? Why do you use them?

2. Do you consider the Bible "God-breathed"? If so, why? What exactly does that term mean to you?

3. How does thinking about the motivations of each biblical writer enhance your understanding and appreciation of the story?

4. Pick a favorite story from the Bible and reimagine it from the perspective of a woman in the story (or even an anonymous female bystander to the story). How might that woman have told the story differently? How might modern readers think of the story had it been written by that woman?

5. How should we read scriptures reflecting the values of ancient cultures (for example, patriarchy, slavery, or polygamy) in light of the values we hold today? What are some potential effects of considering those texts infallible?

2

Two Creation Stories
and Other Myths

The title of this chapter might be a bit unsettling for some readers, as it not only claims that there are two creation stories, instead of just one, but also indicates that there are myths within the Bible. I will admit that neither of these ideas sat well with me the first time I heard them. I had always thought of creation as one seamless story, and the mere mention of "myth" and Bible in the same sentence was nothing short of heretical.

The word *myth* had negative connotations for me, as if it were a story of nothing but pure lies. But a myth is a story that was written to help explain a natural phenomenon or a cultural practice or belief. A simple example of this is the explanation given for rainbows in Genesis 9:8–17. For anyone who thinks of the biblical stories as having literally taken place, seeing a different purpose for the story can be a bit tricky. But I assure you that it is worth the effort to do so.

Take a few moments to take stock of your thoughts about the story of creation, as found at the beginning of Genesis. Imagine you are telling the story to someone hearing it for the first time. Which elements are essential in it? Are Adam and Eve a part of "the" creation story? Are there a certain number of days involved? You get the idea.

(Pause to reflect.)

What most of us think of as being in "the" creation story is actually a combination of details from the two that are in there. Read through Genesis 1–2 for yourself and answer the questions in the following chart.

Chart 1: Comparing Creation Stories

	Genesis 1:1–2:4a (the first half of v. 4)	Genesis 2:4b–25
What is God called?		
How many days are involved?		
In what order are things created?		
At what point in the process are humans created?		
Why are humans created?		

	Genesis 1:1–2:4a (the first half of v. 4)	Genesis 2:4b–25
What does God use to create the humans?		
At what point in the process are animals created?		
What are humans intended to eat?		
How would you describe the way God relates to creation— removed from it, up close and personal, etc.?		
What is this story intended to explain?		

If you read biblical stories expecting them to tell you exactly what happened, you would have to do some pretty fantastic acrobatics to make it work out that both of these stories are absolutely true to actual events. (For example, were plants and animals created before humans, or after?) This is not to mention the fact that there would not have been a court stenographer present, at the time of creation. If you read these stories as myths, as I suggest they were intended to be read, then you are free to take a step back and observe what it is that the storytellers were trying to convey. Reading the Bible "literally" is not necessarily the best way to honor it.

People are often surprised to realize that God is given two different names in Genesis 1 and 2: God and LORD God. This is not due to some conspiracy by the people who translate the Bible into English. "God" in the first story and "LORD God" in the second are used consistently in the Hebrew. The different names indicate that the stories are told by two different storytellers or groups of people.

Let's talk about the way the stories are told. The first story is rather orderly. In that account, God speaks, something comes into being, God sees that it is good, and there is evening and there is morning: day one (or two, or three, etc.). I like to picture God in Genesis 1 standing offstage with a microphone, booming the lines, "Let there be . . . ." In speaking things into being, instead of being right in our midst, God comes across as somewhat removed. Theologians describe this representation of God as *transcendent*.

In the second story, LORD God creates things in a slightly different order than what we see in Genesis 1. There are no days delineated in this account, and LORD God does not speak things into being. This account could almost start with "Once upon a time . . . ." Here, LORD God seems to be right in the middle of things, even using hands (does God actually have physical form?) to scoop up dirt and breathe the breath of life into a human being. LORD God is described as much more present than the "God" of Genesis 1. Theologians call this representation of God as *immanent*. So, even just at the level of the way God is named and talked about, we can see two different ideas at work, consistently, in these two creation stories.

In the first story, male and female humans are created simultaneously, both "in God's image." But in the second, a single human is formed first, then all the animals, then the companion human being. The first story is rather formulaic and repetitive, which makes the story easier to repeat over and over with some accuracy. The second story is more of a narrative, like a story you would read to a child at bedtime. If we let the traits of each story come into focus, it becomes easier to see how it is that we were not meant to read Genesis 1–2 as one continuous story but as two, which happen to be placed next to each other in Genesis. It also helps us to see what many faithful readers of scripture have concluded over the years, which is that these two stories come from different authors or different collections of stories passed along.

Do Vegans Have It "Right"?!

As an interesting aside, in Genesis 1:29–30 it appears that God intends for both the humans' and the animals' food to be the fruits of trees and the vegetation on earth. There is no mention of people eating meat. It is not until Genesis 4 that God "allows" humans to kill animals for food.

I know very few Christians who eat a strict vegan diet, yet that was the first diet mentioned in scripture. This becomes a simple way of highlighting that many people do a great deal of picking and choosing of which biblical passages to follow. Of course, some people will say that the later idea or command from God is what "counts." But they are both still in there. A vegan diet and an omnivore diet are both "biblical."

Let's discuss the reasons given for creating the humans in the first place. They are slightly different, though perhaps not incompatibly so. In the first story, God creates humanity last, after all other forms of life on the planet. Then God gives them dominion over everything on earth, and tells them to be fruitful and multiply and fill the earth. This appears to be the purpose for humans, according to Genesis 1.

The reason for humans in the second account is a bit less clear. In Genesis 2:7, LORD God creates a generic human being (not a male, just a human), and then LORD God creates all the plants. In 2:15, LORD God puts the human in this garden God has created in order for the human to till it and keep it. Notice the boundary that is imposed on the human. In the first story, there is an idea of "the world is your oyster," but in Genesis 2, there are clear delineations in terms of where the human being can go. Then in 2:18, we see that the LORD God does not want this human to be alone, which is why a partner equal to him needs to be created. It is in the search for this partner that LORD

God creates all the animals. Chapter 2 of Genesis ends with the brief announcement, "for this reason" humans pair up and start their own families, in their own homes.

I have heard at least one effort to read Genesis 1–2 as one single story, and it is a fairly popular one. It goes something like this: in Genesis 1, God is just creating the spiritual form or example of the humans. It says that God created them "in his image," and the only way that humans can "look" like God would be on a spiritual level. Then the physical form of humans is created in Genesis 2:5–25. This is a clever reading, I will admit, but it does not address all the other differences in the stories. I would prefer not to call them "contradictions," since

A Generic Earthling and Its Suitable Partner

It is often quite helpful for people to understand some of what is happening in the Hebrew in Genesis 2:7–25. This section is one of those passages where a great deal is lost or gained "in translation."

First, we lose a fun play on words in the Hebrew in Genesis 2:7. My English translation says that the LORD God creates "man from the dust of the ground." But in the Hebrew, ha-'adam is created from ha-'adamah. Ha-'adamah means earth or dirt. Thus, the LORD God uses dirt to create a dirt-being, or earthling, if you will.

The fact that we have chosen to call this first being "Adam," translate ha-'adam as "man," and use male pronouns gives the impression that it was male. But it is not until the second human is created in Genesis 2:22 that the Hebrew storyline uses words for male and female. When there is only one, it is a generic human. (Elsewhere in the Bible, we tend to translate ha-'adam as generically human, not specifically male.) Once there are two humans, the idea of male- and femaleness is introduced. In other words, we have reason to stop saying that "Man was created first, and then Woman from his rib."

Second, notice how the second human is talked about. One translation of Genesis 2:18 (NRSV) says, "Then the LORD God said, 'It is not good that the human should be alone; I will make him a helper as his partner.'" What connotations does the word helper have for you? For many people, the word means "subordinate" or "servant," suggesting that woman was made for man's benefit, in order to complete him.

What we see, if we look at the Hebrew terms, however, is a bit more of a partner-on-equal-grounds idea. The first Hebrew word here is 'ezer, which is not a common term in the Bible. Elsewhere, it is used to describe a foreign nation coming to the rescue of the Israelites, or God himself as the helper or savior of his people. The writer of some of the psalms calls out to God, his helper in his time of need. Notice the connotations of strength rather than subordination? It does not make much sense, then, to render 'ezer differently here just because it refers to a human that turns out to be female.

The term translated as "suitable for him" comes from the compound word, kanegdo, which literally means "as before him." Think of "before him" as meaning face-to-face. In that culture, one looked only an equal in the eye. This "helper" is to be someone on equal footing; they are to look eye-to-eye with each other.

Many people have it so deeply engrained in their minds that women were created to supplement or complement men that they cannot see that this idea is, in part, based on unfortunate translation choices in this verse or two. Can you imagine all that would be gained if we could correct this misunderstanding?

that term implies that one version is correct in depicting the world's origins and the other is not. In the true sense of myths, it is okay that there are differences in these stories, because they are trying to convey very different aspects of who God was to those people or are addressing different unexplainable elements of their world.

The last question on the chart asks what it is that each creation story was intended to explain. This is not meant to be a trick question. Rather, it is pushing you to look deeper than "it describes where the world came from." Myths were written in order to explain something: a cultural practice, a natural phenomenon, or an aspect of life that causes a child to ask, "How come?" We show respect to the scriptures, as well as to their authors and the communities that passed them along, when we read Genesis 1–2 with this in mind.

Often, the main point becomes clear at the end of the story. This is true for both creation stories in Genesis. For instance, Genesis 2:2–3 (the end of the first creation story) says, "So God blessed the seventh day and hallowed it, because on it God rested from all the work that he had done in creation." The storyteller is letting us know that one of the many things this story was intended to explain is why it is that the Israelites take a day of rest every week. This cultural practice attracted criticism, so having a myth that explains where it came from—it was first done by their God—justifies the practice. It also gives the adults a story to tell their children that helps them pass along the practice.

At the end of the second creation story, in 2:24–25, we have a "therefore," which is a clue to stop to see what it is there for. "Therefore a man leaves his father and his mother and clings to his wife, and they become one flesh. And the man and his wife were both naked, and were not ashamed." When we read attentively, we can see that some of the wording indicates that people were concerned about their children leaving home and creating bonds and their own families with someone

---

Sex without Marriage

There is a tidbit in 2:24–25 that I would encourage you to give open, honest consideration. All English translations, except for the Contemporary English Version, use "the man and his wife" in these two verses, instead of what would be more consistent: the man and his woman. This is a small distinction, but let's take a moment to think through its far-reaching implications.

When we render Genesis 2:24 as, "Therefore a man leaves his father and mother and clings to his wife, and the two become one flesh," we are suggesting that a marriage has taken place. Throughout the centuries, people in the Church have insisted, based on this translation, that marriage itself is ordained by God. Part of the issue is that *ishshah* can be translated as "woman" or "wife," and the same goes for *ish*: "man" or "husband."

If we render Genesis 2:24 a bit more consistently, it would say, "Therefore a man (*ish*) leaves his father and mother and clings to his woman (*ishshah*), and the two become one flesh." Admittedly, this is still focused on the man, and he still gets to acquire a woman, very much like property. But this translation focuses on the fact that people pair up, and it is explaining why people grow up, leave home, and strike out on their own. This focus is quite different from claiming that Genesis 2:24 tells us that God intends marriage and that it is only between a man and a woman.

Interestingly enough, there are plenty of examples of "biblical marriage," especially in the Hebrew Bible, that many people today do not approve of, or perhaps are unaware of (see chap. 4 for further discussion). For instance, polygamy is not only an example of biblical marriage, it is essential for the building of the Israelite people. There is levirate marriage, where a man must marry (or just have sex with) his dead brother's widow and have children who are attributed to the first husband. Then there are biblical laws that endorse forcing a woman to marry her rapist. These and other eye-opening examples of "biblical marriage" we are probably better off not enforcing today. But they are all discussing the issue of marriage and what it looked like, at that time.

This one verse, Genesis 2:24, has been a "go to" verse on marriage, however, even though the Hebrew does not warrant it. In fact, one could say that this is an example of a bit of conspiracy on the part of biblical translation committees, since all but one chose to render it, "a man and his wife." Many people are taught this skewed rendering so well that they expend a great deal of energy trying to defend it, and they insist that this passage is proof that sex before marriage is a sin. In fact, this passage suggests that in having sex, two people become married. I am glad that we do not see things this way, today, but it is important to be aware of what the biblical story is saying, on its own terms.

else. Remember, this story is about origins. It is addressing why we have the urges or desires to partner up. It is not talking about the contributions we all seek to make to society in general. Thus, when people (mis)read this story and take this idea of a woman completing a man as the reason God created women, they cut off worlds of possibility from women. Perhaps it is done unintentionally or unconsciously, but doing so actually belittles a part of God's creation.

Again, I would encourage you to stop and reflect on how much of a difference translation can make. Think about the worlds of difference between the two meanings of the story that I have discussed here: thinking of women as subordinate to men and created to complete them versus thinking of this story as giving a reason as to why we desire to partner up and strike out on our own. The distinctions in meanings that come from the translations are not always as significant as what we see here. Regardless, I hope you will pause and think for yourself about how much a slight rewording has perhaps surprised you or caused you to see this story differently than you did before.

What does this tell you about the power of those who produce the translations? What does this tell you about the power a phrase has, simply for being within the Bible? Think about the power a particular interpretation has had, since it was drawn on for centuries by the men within the Church who taught people what to believe. I invite you to think about the fact that millions of people are actually more influenced today by the translation choices of men of the early Church than by a faithful rendering of this particular passage. Many people today, who are claiming to believe a face-value reading of scripture, are actually taking a misinterpretation of this story at face value instead.

I can imagine that some of you might be thinking to yourself, "Well of course she would want to see it this way; she is a woman!" You would be absolutely correct. I am a female, and I do want to see this story as talking about why people desire to partner up. I absolutely do want people to stop using it to put women in a subordinate position to men. Yes, this women-were-created-to-be-subordinate-to-men meaning has been used against me and countless other women in my life, not to mention against millions of other women over the centuries. My desire to have this stop should not be seen as a strike against me, though. You do not have to be a woman to want this subordinating interpretation to cease to be applied. Empowering all people, and not just men, is better for everyone. It is not such a terrible and ungodly thing for people to desire to be all they were created to be.

MYTHS AROUND THE WORLD

The comparison of biblical stories to Greek mythology can often feel a bit unsettling. Many people within the Church think of the stories in the Bible as being true in a unique way and similarly think that the stories in ancient mythologies are mere stories. For them, there is a qualitative difference. I suggest that they be seen as on the same plane, however, just for different cultures.

There are "creation stories" or creation myths for many cultures around the world. Each of them is particular to that geographical location, incorporating the natural phenomena or cultural practices of that region. People in New Zealand would understandably have a reason to "explain" why there are tsunamis. An Australian myth might give the origin of kangaroos. People who grow up close to the poles of the planet would quite reasonably have cold weather or ice formations play a central role in the creation of things. People who have to contend with bears might want to have a story to tell their children, in terms of the reason God or the gods would place something so dangerous and scary in their midst.

Most of these creation myths will also address things such as how humans are to relate to deity and how God created humans. Strikingly, many of them also connect humans to the earth, quite literally: God formed them from mud, or they fall out of pea pods, and so forth. Many students have asked, in response to this last idea, "Do they really believe humans came from a pea pod?!" There is an odd irony in this sincere question, since that same student might believe that God literally formed the first human from dirt. The difference is that this student grew up with the Genesis 2 idea, not the pea pod one, so being formed from dirt seems normal and realistic.

If you are a person who thinks it is impossible for an educated adult to believe that humans were initially formed from dirt, as Genesis 2 suggests, I am here to tell you that it is indeed not impossible. Many people do believe that very thing. The idea that "with God, anything is possible" is applied to this kind of a situation, allowing people to believe in something biologically impossible. It is a good thing to be aware of the power these scriptures have for people. Instead of dismissing someone whose beliefs seem outlandish to you, perhaps you will pause and consider where those beliefs come from and what is at stake for that person to hold onto them.

CONCLUSION

Talking about myths in the Bible and two creation stories in Genesis is not intended to challenge anyone's faith. If that is one of the side effects, as it initially was for me, then take heart in knowing that the Bible itself has not changed, just your perspective on it. If we read these two chapters of Genesis looking for what it is that the authors were trying to explain, instead of expecting the stories to have actually taken place, the stories themselves become much more interesting!

Now that we have discussed how to understand these two stories as "myths," you can apply a similar engagement with other myths in the Bible. You can keep on reading up through Genesis 11. All the stories in this segment of the Bible qualify as what we call primeval history. They are stories that were written about the origins of many aspects of the culture and worldview of the people of Israel. The stories will make more sense if we read with these ideas about myths in mind, looking for the messages the authors were trying to impart.

 TAKE THE BIBLE INTO YOUR OWN HANDS

1. Does the technical definition of the word *myth* differ from how you typically have defined it? Do you see myths in the Bible as different from myths of other cultures?

2. Tell the story of Genesis 1 in your own words. Then tell the story of Genesis 2. Did telling each story separately make anything stand out for you? What differences did you notice as you told each story?

3. What are some implications of the way we typically talk about "the" creation story? How would cultural debates on biology and human origins be different if we talked about the differences between Genesis 1 and 2 and their reasons for having been written?

4. Given the difference translating just one word (such as *man/human* or *woman/wife*) differently can make in our interpretation of the story, how much authority do you think we can give scriptures translated from their original languages?

5. Imagine some of the passages in Genesis 1–11 as answers to a child's question. For example, "Papa, why do we have to work so hard to grow food?" (see Gen. 3:17–19). What questions might children have asked that prompted someone to tell the stories in Genesis 2:21–24 and 11:1–9?

3

What Really Happened in the Garden?

The ideas associated with Genesis 3, the "Adam and Eve" story, are perhaps the most popular of any biblical story (aside from Jesus') in the Western world today. The ideas of Adam-as-first-man, the apple as a symbol of temptation, "original sin," or Eve-as-seductress play well in our media and advertising. There is the chain lingerie store named Adam and Eve®, which has a tagline: "America's most trusted source for adult products," and a logo of a bitten-into apple. The not-so-subtle marketing and advertising for the show "Desperate Housewives" consistently used Eve, an apple, seduction, and the color red. There are countless references to Adam and Eve in secular music. Even the general idea of "blaming Eve" is so popular that a bumper sticker, "Eve was framed," has been gracing the backs of cars for years.

Then there are all the examples that focus on the snake or serpent as some form of tempter. My favorite of these is an early advertisement for Absolut® Pear, in which a snake slithers around the Absolut bottle, with a pear shape protruding from its middle. Ap"pear"antly, this flavor of Absolut isss ssssimply too tempting to withsssstand.

But there are also a few examples that play with the idea of knowledge gained, in a positive way. My favorite of these examples is the *Bizarro* cartoon, by Dan Piraro, of a subtly naked woman sitting next to an Apple® computer, the apple-with-a-bite-missing logo displayed, and a snake wrapped around the trunk of a tree saying, "Of course he told you not to touch it—then you'd have access to all the data he does." Sometimes it is hard to believe how widely applied this story is.

Before reading any further, take a few moments to collect your own thoughts regarding what the story of "the Garden of Eden" is telling us. What are the crucial aspects of this story? Who does what, and why is any of it an issue? Who is the "evil" character in the story? What is the "moral of this story"?

If you have thought of this story as only being about "original sin" or "the fall of Man," you are in for quite a ride. So, hold on to your hat and buckle your seatbelt.

READING GENESIS 3 WITH FRESH EYES

Given this story's placement at the beginning of the Bible, and the way that early Christian thought drew on this story as the moment things went awry, it is no wonder that so many people of faith see it as an essential component of their view of human nature.

In order to get a fresh perspective on this story, you need to keep in mind what it means that it is an honest-to-goodness myth. Remember, a myth is a story that explains a natural phenomenon or a cultural practice. If you approach Genesis 3 with this perspective on myths, you are prepared to ask what it is that this story is explaining or what cultural practice it is justifying. This approach changes, quite significantly, the way a story is read. You are no longer reading it as prescriptive, as something God intended, but rather as descriptive: there is something in our world that needs a backstory, and this is what these ancient people came up with.

Turn to Genesis 3 and read through the chapter for yourself, keeping your curiosity engaged and perhaps pausing to consider parts of the story you have never noticed before. The first line is one such possible moment. It says that the serpent (notice that it never says "Satan") was the craftiest animal that God had created. Being crafty is not the same thing as being deceitful. It might even give a nod toward the necessity of the serpent's role. Whatever the case, I hope you will try to read through this story without jumping to any conclusions. Just let the story unfold.

Do you notice the bits of exaggeration, perhaps for dramatic effect, in the woman's comments? But does the serpent say anything deceitful? No, it does not. It was Paul, in the Newer Testament, who has led many of us to believe it did: "But I am afraid that as the serpent deceived Eve by its cunning . . . ." (2 Cor. 11:3). In fact, if you pay close attention to Genesis 2–3, you will see that it is actually God who has misled the humans, not the serpent. Hmmm.

If you read this story as if it actually happened, I have just called God a liar. If you read it as a myth, then what the story attributes to God—in this case some sketchy, misleading commands—is not such a big deal. Reading it as a myth means reading for the bigger meaning more than the details.

Did you catch what the woman notices about the tree in Genesis 3:6? She noticed that the "tree was desired to make one wise." In fact, the knowledge of good and evil is something we consider to be an essential aspect of being a responsible adult. Is it not? There are three groups of people that I know of who do not have this kind of knowledge: infants, some people whose mental capacities are rather limited, and sociopaths. Well, perhaps sociopaths have this knowledge, they just do not care about it. But you get the point.

Taking the intention of a myth, I would suggest that this passage is trying to explain why we, as humans, have this particular knowledge of "good and evil" and other animals seemingly do not. Speaking for myself, I am thankful that, metaphorically speaking, the female was interested in more knowledge. I'm glad she took that bite. Life would be much less interesting and less technologically evolved if we all lived in an infantile bliss (or much worse if the world was full of apathetic sociopaths!).

Notice how the story says that the two humans' "eyes were opened" (v. 7). When people read this story literally, they think that there was a time in history when humans did not have this awareness or consciousness. When read as a myth, it is merely trying to give a story to explain why we do. Do you see the difference?

Other fascinating elements of this chapter of Genesis include the "punishments" given in 3:16–19. Genesis 3:16:

> "I will greatly increase your pangs in childbearing;
>   in pain you shall bring forth children,
> yet your desire shall be for your husband,
>   and he shall rule over you."

From a literal perspective, if God chose to do this to women then God is a bit . . . well, sadistic. Additionally, the second part of the verse tells us that in spite of the pain of pushing a baby out of an impossibly

Satan

While so many of us assume the devil or Satan is featured in Genesis 3, in fact the earliest writing in the Bible in which we see a character called "satan" is the book of Job (see chap. 6 for more on Job). In context, you can tell that he is one of several of God's advisors, who, incidentally, are called "sons of God" (Job 1:6). Much like "Adam" in Genesis 2, whose name comes from turning the Hebrew word *ha-adam* into a proper name, we have given Satan this name based on the Hebrew for his role, *ha-satan*.

The footnotes on Job 1:6 often say that we could also call Satan the "accuser" or "adversary." Whatever our dictionaries might suggest to us, it is worth looking at what is happening in the story and then perhaps deciding what you think this character is doing. If you read this passage carefully, *ha-satan* is not really accusing anyone of anything. *Ha-satan*'s role in the story is more like what we call a "devil's advocate," which is no coincidence, given this is the story from which we get this idea. Being a "devil's advocate" means that you point out a perspective in a situation in order to see it more clearly. In the opening scene of the book of Job, God is quite pleased with Job's devotion. *Ha-satan* merely suggests that if you take away all of Job's abundance, he would probably no longer be so devoted to God.

In the book of Job, *ha-satan*'s role is over at the end of chapter 2; he is not the one who inflicts all the suffering on Job. There is a later version of this story (*The Testament of Job*) in which Satan is depicted as testing Job, but that version is not in the Bible.

There are actually very few references to "Satan" in the Hebrew Bible. *Ha-satan* plays the "devil's advocate" in Job, gets a quick plug for inciting David into doing something he should not have done in 1 Chronicles 21:1, and has a bizarre cameo in Zechariah 3:1–2. This is not much playing time, which tells us how little the writers of the Hebrew Bible thought about *ha-satan*.

The appearances of Satan in the Newer Testament are a different matter. The role of this creature might surprise you. Looking at the Gospels, Matthew 4:1–11 (the same as Mark 1:12–13 and Luke 4:1–13) has the story of Jesus being tested in the wilderness. This is quite similar to the early tests that many heroes throughout the ancient world went through, before being sent on their missions. You, the reader, need to be assured that the hero is up for the task ahead. Imagine, if you will, Satan looking up into the sky after the third test, giving God the two thumbs up signal. "He's good to go!" This view of Satan suggests he has an important role, rather than that he is just testing Jesus because he's a jerk.

I hope that this Satan-had-an-important-role possibility will stay in the back of your mind as you read other Newer Testament passages that mention him. People talk about this character in such negative terms, but the combination of ideas associated with Satan is far more complex and was developed over hundreds of years. Satan as the embodiment of evil is a more recent development.

Read and consider some of the other Newer Testament passages where Satan is mentioned (Matt. 12:26, 16:23; Mark 4:15; Luke 10:18, Luke 22; 1 Cor. 5:5; 1 Thess. 2:18). For more on this topic, I suggest that you look at related entries in the *Anchor Bible Dictionary* or Elaine Pagels' *The Origin of Satan*.

---

small passage, women will still desire sex with their husbands, and that those husbands will rule over them. Note how starkly different this is from what we see in Genesis 2:18, where the two humans are described as partners and equals.

Go back to reading the whole passage as a myth. Verse 16 offers an explanation for why childbirth is painful. In spite of humans needing and being drawn to each other as suggested in Genesis 2:18, there are dynamics between men and women that have developed over time that are difficult to explain. Genesis 3:16 gives some "backstory" to them. It does not have to be the final word, however.

A book by Leonard Shlain, *Sex, Time and Power: How Women's Sexuality Shaped Human Evolution,* showed me a delightful connection between the desire to create a myth about the pain of childbirth and the fact that homo sapiens are physiologically different from four-legged and arms-to-the-ground animals. Being physically upright means that homo sapiens' pelvic girdle must be tight so that it will hold the fetus in as it develops and gets heavier. In other animals, the pelvic girdle does not have to have such a narrow opening, since the mother leans forward or is carrying the developing young in a complete dangle-type position. Our uprightness explains the pain that human females experience in childbirth, as compared to this process for other animals. It makes sense to me that some ancient peoples wanted a story to "explain" this reality.

Something similar can be said about the "punishment" given to the man. It seems rather silly to suggest that a loving God would choose to make it quite difficult for humans to scrape together enough food to eat. But if this is the reality that some humans were facing and they believed in a good and loving God who provided for them, then it makes sense that they would create a story to try to explain why this tension exists.

Also keep in mind that there is not a reference to "sin" in this story, nor is it necessary to see this event as a "fall." Some rabbis and pastors see the enlightenment and awareness in this story as a "step up" for humankind.

If we read this story as a myth, we do not have to perpetuate an idea that God chose to make life difficult for us in response to us being the curious human beings we were created to be. Instead, we can see Genesis 3 for what it was originally trying to do: explain challenging physiological and agricultural realities and the complexities that come from having a conscience.

When we read this story and hold onto the details as if they all actually happened, we end up establishing a starting point between God and humans that is tricky, at best, to negotiate down the road. The early Church Fathers offer us their conclusions about the God-human relationship, almost entirely based on reading Genesis 3 as if it actually happened. Now that you know that there is another way to read Genesis 3, see what you think of their conclusions.

CHURCH FATHERS READING GENESIS 3

One of the most eye-opening aspects of seminary for me was learning some of what a handful of men thought and wrote over the past 1,900 years and realizing that many of their ideas are still alive today. Furthermore, I was shocked to see how often those ideas are not backed up by scripture, but rather, were read into scripture. The way many people read Genesis 3 today is influenced more by the Church Fathers' ideas than by what is contained in the story itself.

Tertullian, at the beginning of the third century, claimed that the devil was jealous of humanity, since God had put everything under their watch instead of under the devil's care. Tertullian then suggests that the devil deceived the man, but that it was when the devil spoke with the woman that he managed to infect them both with the spirit of discontent. This is what led her to sin and to lead the man into sinning as well. Tertullian claims that this act is the source of all judgment and sin. Furthermore, prior to these actions, the humans were blameless, but in ceasing to be content with how things were, the humans no longer cared for God or heavenly things (*de patientia*, V:5–14).

Note that Tertullian talks about the devil being in these stories, even though the Bible does not. It's an interesting idea he had that the devil spoke to the man first but wasn't able to persuade him, isn't it? Additionally, nowhere in Genesis 1–3 does it say anything about the humans no longer caring for God or heavenly things. All these claims by Tertullian reflect a great deal of reading into scripture, yet Tertullian is commended in the Church tradition for his use of scripture. Hmmm.

Next we have Origen, also in the third century, from whom we get the first glimpse about sinfulness being tied to sex. Though he is not drawing specifically on Genesis 3, Origen claims that all people born into this world are contaminated by both mother and father. This contamination is due to gestating in our mothers' wombs and from getting from our fathers' sperm all that is needed for our bodies to form, since this is how they believed things worked (*Homilia in Leviticum*, xii). Take a few moments to think about these two claims. Would these presuppositions hold up today?

The idea of sex being linked to sinfulness is important to understand because it is an essential component for justifying the belief that Jesus was conceived without intercourse (see chap. 8). God, not a male human, helped Mary conceive so Jesus did not have sinfulness from his father. In terms of explaining why Mary did not contaminate Jesus, the *Protevangelium of James* says that Mary was also miraculously conceived. This allowed her to be "pure" enough to be chosen to carry Jesus in her womb. According to Origen, "Only Jesus my Lord was born without stain. He was not polluted in respect to his mother, for he entered a body which was not contaminated. . . . For Joseph played no part in his birth other than his devotion and affection" (*Homilia in Leviticum* xii, 4). Notice how intercourse is thought to cause a woman's body to be contaminated.

Augustine's contributions on several theological topics have held sway over the centuries. He wrote hundreds of pages about the Trinity, humanity, sin, grace, and free will. It appears that at times he reads Genesis 2–3 as literally having happened, since he claims that prior to the serpent having a conversation with Eve, humans were sinless and blissfully ignorant. He says that our guilty nature is due to this original sin, and it deserves a just penalty. Augustine even took it to the step that we, as humans, are deserving only of death and God's wrath, and that any mercy we have been given, including salvation, we have not deserved.

Does this make any of you wonder about Augustine's childhood? I am actually not joking around on this one. I'm not sure which part makes me more sad: that he took the guilt and punishment bit to a whole new level or that other men of the early Church ended up agreeing with him!

It seems that some of the beliefs about human sinfulness that the Church teaches are based on ideas that have been read into this passage, and yet still depend on it actually having taken place. It is quite an interesting situation, wouldn't you say?

This Made Pelagius a Heretic?

Pelagius, a contemporary of Augustine, held beliefs on sin, human nature, and grace that stood counter to Augustine's. Many of his beliefs were deemed heretical in the Council of Carthage in 418. Two of them are pertinent to this discussion: "Even if Adam had not sinned, he would have died," and "Adam's sin harmed only himself, not the human race." While I still do not read Genesis 3 as being about "sin," I appreciate his point that "original sin" is not really a thing, and it is certainly not passed along like a genetic disorder. These two claims of his, among many others, were deemed to be not just wrong but heretical. The men at that council pronounced that holding Pelagius's beliefs meant a person would be anathematized: cursed or condemned, and cut off from the Church.

Many of Augustine's thoughts, which endorse a strikingly negative view of humans and a frightfully angry God, were embraced as reasonable and theologically sound.

Circling back around to where this chapter began, there is a newer advertisement for Absolut® Pear that alludes to a vagina (I'm not making this up!), suggesting that female sexuality is the ultimate temptation, or perhaps second only to their vodka. Something tells me that this offshoot from the earlier version, mentioned at the beginning of this chapter, would be just fine with the Church Fathers.

Whatever the case, there is a radical difference between the mythic purpose of the story contained in Genesis 3 and what people have done with it and read into it over the years. It breaks my heart to see how much of what has been imposed on this story is negative about or detrimental to human relations, and entirely unnecessarily! Think about it. Permission granted.

 ## TAKE THE BIBLE INTO YOUR OWN HANDS

1. What ideas about the Garden story did you grow up with? How has Genesis 3 influenced how you think about human relationship with God?

2. Why do you think it made sense to the early Church Fathers to interpret Adam and Eve's "temptation" as being about sex instead of acquiring knowledge? What is your response to Origen's idea that the reason all people are born sinful is due to the procreative act?

3. Do you consider *ha-satan* ("Satan") the embodiment of evil? Looking at Job 1–2 or Matthew 4, do you think that perspective is justified in scripture?

4. Do you think Pelagius was heretical for saying that Adam's sin did not make the rest of humanity sinful? There is a good deal of Church doctrine built on the idea that "in Adam all have sinned." How does it change things for you knowing that there was not total agreement on these important ideas?

5. How might things be different if we gave up the idea of "original sin" and celebrated Eve's courage for desiring more knowledge instead?

4

Sex: Who, What, and Why?

Sex and sexuality are fascinating topics. They are often the subject of jokes, and certainly most people find some pleasure in the acts. But they are also difficult to discuss in a serious way. What a curious thing. Something so central to our humanity, and necessary to perpetuate humankind, practically takes on taboo status in the realm of conversation. Additionally, when it comes to discussing "what the Bible says on it," many people have limited or misinformed perspectives. So it might not surprise you to learn that this is my favorite topic to discuss: What does the Bible say about sex and sexuality?

WHO

Naturally, this category overlaps with the "what" and "why" sections. While it might seem a bit ridiculous to focus on the "who" of it, it is informative to look at who the Bible discusses or acknowledges as being able to have sex.

Heterosexual Sex

Of course husbands and wives are expected to engage in this activity, since it is necessary for procreation. But when it comes to biblical ideals about marriage, and thus husband and wife combinations, there are some categories that were normal at the time that many people raise an eyebrow at today. So, since part of the question about "who gets to have sex" is answered by looking at marriage in the Bible, let's take a look at what marriage and its counterpart, "adultery," actually look like in the Bible.

"Biblical Marriage"

If someone says that she supports only "biblical marriage," what kind of a marriage do you think she is referring to? I usually take it as a reference to marriage between one man and one woman, perhaps with some disdain for divorce. "Biblical marriage," however, is a far cry from marriages based on mutual love and respect, as we expect today, and the "Christ-centered" marriage was not even Jesus' idea. In fact, Jesus' words about marriage might shock you. So let's begin with what we see in the Hebrew Bible.

There are plenty of man/woman couples discussed in the Hebrew Bible. The stories of some of the biggies—Adam and Eve, Isaac and Rebekah, Abraham and Sarah—never mention a wedding. This is, in part, because the wedding event as we know it had not yet developed. At the time, a man went out, found a woman he wanted to marry, purchased her from her father, and took her home as his wife. Done and done. Because women were viewed and valued differently at the time than they typically are today, women were not consulted in this exchange. Biblically speaking, a woman rarely had a voice. This reality, alone, ought to make us pause and think before passing along an idea simply because it comes from the Bible.

To that point, polygamy was practiced by several of the patriarchs in the Bible. (Joseph Smith drew on scripture to justify the practice as a part of Mormonism.) Jacob is the man who fathered the twelve sons, whose descendants made up the twelve tribes of Israel. But Jacob had four women making the babies for him. Two of those women were his wives (simultaneously), and two were his wives' slaves. Polygamy/ open-marriage-for-the-man was an acceptable standard for "biblical marriage."

Other examples of marriage in the Hebrew Bible include a woman and her rapist (Deut. 22:28–29). You see, a woman's worth was based on two things: her sexual purity prior to marriage and her ability to produce sons. So if a woman is raped she is no longer a virgin, which is tragic . . . for her father. That's right. The issue is not about the harm done to her. She loses some of her market value; she is considered "tainted." Though it might sound harsh to us, a woman's virginity wasn't so much about virtue as ownership. No man wanted a woman that some other man had "had." So the rapist had an obligation to keep the woman he had violated as his wife and to pay her father the bride price for a virgin.

Daughters were given as rewards for succeeding in battle (Josh. 15:16), and marriages were one means of making alliances between two groups of people (2 Chr. 18:1). Marriages were to be strictly between two people of Israel. Men were not to give their daughters away to men who were not Israelites, neither were they to take non-Israelites as wives for their sons (Ezra 9:12; Neh. 10:30). This is an issue that comes up a great deal; apparently the Israelites had a hard time playing by these rules. However racist this may sound to us today, it was important for the Israelites to maintain a sense of purity of the people of God. It is these commands that Christians used to back legislation making inter-racial marriages illegal in the United States.

Then there is the levirate marriage scenario. This is the rule that when a man dies without having any male children to carry on his name, it is up to his brother to marry (or just have sex with) the widow and have children with her. Those children were thought to belong to the first husband. I have found that men with brothers do not always find this practice very appealing nowadays!

There are examples of keeping foreign women as booty after sacking a town. It is not clear if these women would then be seen as wives or concubines or just as slaves (Num. 31:1–18; Deut. 21:11–14). We might assume that they are slaves or concubines, since a righteous Israelite wouldn't marry foreign women. Regardless, she was property that was available for sexual encounters.

These are all views of how men could engage in sex or marriage within the Hebrew Bible. Marriage, as talked about in the Newer Testament, is similarly not so simple or straightforward.

For instance, Jesus shows approval of marriage by attending a wedding in John 2. But he also talks about leaving all of one's possessions behind, including families, in order to follow him (Luke 18:28–30). Jesus does not seem to have a problem with levirate marriage (see "Jesus on Levirate Marriage" below). He also never refers to a wife of his own, which does seem odd for a guy his age. Or it could be because he had a preference for celibacy. Jesus had some pretty extreme positions on divorce, which some denominations cling to quite tightly, to this day. Matthew 5:31–32 says that if anyone gets divorced for any reason except for "unchastity" and then remarries he or she is committing adultery. This is striking, to me, in that the focus is on the sex act, not on the relationships involved. Insisting that divorce is "wrong," based on scripture, must uphold the idea that sex marks someone's territory.

Jesus on Levirate Marriage

There is a scene in the Gospels where Jesus is questioned about levirate marriage, not for its morality but for its connection to the resurrection (see Matt. 22:23–33; Mark 12:18–27). The Sadducees chose the topic since they did not believe in the resurrection but other Jews did. They propose the scenario of one woman marrying seven brothers and ask whose wife she would be at the resurrection. Jesus replies that no one will be married at the resurrection, so their hypothetical question doesn't disprove the resurrection as they'd hoped. I mention this story because Jesus' response seems to indicate that he does not question the practice of levirate marriage. Either way, it was still a practice at that point in time and not just a Hebrew Bible issue. Levirate marriage might also be the issue for "the woman at the well," in John 4. Many people, on hearing that she had been married to five men and was living with a sixth, conclude something negative about her sexual conduct. Given that women were at the mercy of the men in their lives, perhaps we should see her as a victim instead of as a "loose woman." She would not have had the power to divorce her husband, much less five of them. Either way, Jesus did not seem to judge her actions in the least.

What is rarely referenced in this conversation, however, is Jesus' endorsement of castration (Matt. 19:9–12). When he makes the claim that divorcing and then remarrying is committing adultery, his disciples respond as if that standard is so high that it is better not to marry in the first place. Note Jesus' response: he does not talk them off their ledge! Rather, he simply suggests that being (or making oneself) a eunuch for the sake of the kingdom is a high calling for those who can handle it. "Let anyone accept this who can" (19:12). Think about what this means for "biblical marriage." Jesus himself suggests that castrated men are of the greatest worth for the kingdom. This does, you must agree, make procreation a bit tricky.

Paul, on the other hand, does directly address marriage a few times, most clearly in 1 Corinthians 7:1–16. What is interesting to note is that the commands or directives he offers regarding marriage are all focused on sex. He is not giving relationship advice, just sex advice. The interesting twist here is that Paul claims to be celibate (1 Cor. 7: 7–8). Why would we want to take sex advice from a man who does not have it and who says that he wishes more people made the same choice?

Regardless, Paul tells couples not to withhold (the sex part is implied) from each other, and he says this to both the man and the woman. He even affirms that women ought to have their own husbands. This is progress to speak about a woman as more than the property of a man! He also says that when married, your spouse has authority over your body, and likewise you do over your spouse's body. Please do stop to think about the implications of this claim. I have seen married people literally flinch out of concern when this line is read out loud. Did Paul have good intentions? Most likely. Does that mean that he was spot on with every piece of advice he offered? No, it does not.

But there is another side to Paul's comments about both partners belonging to each other that I hope you will consider. As we know today, what happens in "the bedroom" is a microcosm of the relationship overall. By insisting that husbands' and wives' bodies belong to each other, Paul affirms equality in marriage. This ideal directly contradicts the view of husbands and wives that we see in the later letters attributed to Paul.

Additionally, Paul's strong suggestion that people remain unmarried (1 Cor. 7:7) was said with the immanent return of the Son of Man in mind and thus was a short-term issue. You might want to ask yourself why, for almost twenty centuries, parts of the Church have held on to the "stay unmarried" ideal, sometimes applied to clergy, in 1 Corinthians 7:7 but not the "equality in marriage" part in 1 Corinthians 7:3–4.

Other ideas about marriage in the Newer Testament, specifically in some of the letters that were written near the end of the first century, tend to reflect a return to more traditional ideals. Apparently, some women who were taking to heart Paul's comment, "I wish that all were as I am" (1 Cor. 7:7), had begun choosing not to marry. Socially and politically, there was no acceptable category for a woman who was not married and procreating. Thus, Ephesians 5:21–25 tells wives to be subject to their husbands in all things, just as they are subject to Christ; and the husband is head over his wife as Christ is head over the

Church. In doing these things, Christians would put to rest any suspicions about them being subversive, due to women in leadership and living autonomous lives.

There is a similar command in 1 Timothy 2:15 that makes sense in light of these political ideals. Women in the Jesus movement might be saved from physical persecution and death if they would just adhere to the political ideals of having children and rearing "good citizens." In 1 Peter 3:1–7, the author tells wives to silently accept their husbands' authority. Again, the advice is limited to the "women obey your man" ideal. We see a brief reference in 1 Timothy 3, when describing the qualifications of bishops or deacons, to being married only once. But we cannot tell if the command is about countering polygamy, denouncing levirate marriages, or if it was anti-divorce.

Regardless, we see marriage discussed in the Newer Testament as both something expected of people—and this definitely only between a man and a woman—and the antithesis, as something that you do well to avoid. The most blatant commands to this end come from Jesus and a genuine letter from Paul. It depends on which parts you read, the genuine Paul or the later writers, for determining the woman's property status within a marriage.

All these categories fall under the "biblical marriage" umbrella. Are we supposed to encourage women to see themselves as property, since that is the predominant view of them in the Bible? It is also not just a matter of, "Things changed with Jesus, cancelling out the Hebrew Bible." If we followed Jesus' ideas closely, men would be encouraged to leave their families in order to follow Christ and the most respected men in churches would be those who chose castration.

The next time you hear someone affirm "biblical marriage," why not ask which form of "biblical marriage" the person means? If you're really in for some excitement, ask for passages that back up what they are referring to and discuss freely.

Adultery

The issue of adultery, and how to define it, inevitably comes up when studying the Bible with curious people. The seventh commandment says, "Thou shall not commit adultery" (Exod. 20:14; Deut. 5:18). That seems pretty straightforward. Just do not do it. But what qualifies as adultery, and why it is to be avoided, are not necessarily the same in the Bible as they are today.

According to Leviticus 20:10, adultery is a matter of one man having sex with another man's wife. Whether the man involved in the "affair" was married does not seem to be important. The main reason adultery was wrong was because one man was enjoying another man's property. Please do pause to reflect on this idea.

Jesus is said to have raised the bar, quite a bit, on the topic of adultery, perhaps to such a level that every person with a libido is guilty. Matt. 5:27–30 is a part of the "Sermon on the Mount," where Jesus affirms the Jewish scripture by taking those ideas to a more intense or restrictive level. Instead of "you shall not commit adultery," Jesus claims that having a lustful thought for a woman qualifies as adultery. Whoa! Jesus speaks hyperbolically throughout this section of Matthew, recommending amputating body parts that cause you to sin, so perhaps we should take it all with a grain of salt. Whatever the case, Jesus' redefinition of adultery goes far beyond a typical view of adultery today.

There is an interesting story in John 7:53–8:10 that I invite you to reconsider as well. As you read this story for yourself, imagine the scene playing out in your mind, and pay attention to the way you envision the main characters: Jesus, the unnamed woman, and the temple leaders.

Why do you suppose some people (and Bibles) call it, "The woman caught in adultery"? I thought it takes two for that to happen. Also, how does a group of men just happen to "catch" her in the act, first thing in the morning? Were they spying on her? Was one of the men among them the bait? A woman is used to try to catch Jesus in a bind, legally. She is brought before a crowd, in the temple of all places, perhaps half-dressed. And no one, at the end of the story, apologizes to her! Not even Jesus. Yes, he bends down to write in the dirt, whether as a distraction, or to buy some time, or to list the leaders' sins. He also tells her to go and sin no more. This is, again, an ideal I can affirm in general (though who among us can actually meet that standard?), but takes very little of her personal story into account. Was she married? Was she a prostitute? If by "sinning" he was referring to her day job, or should I say "night job," where else is she then supposed to turn?

So why is the story labelled in such a way that ignores the role of men throughout it? Why not, "Temple leaders frame a woman" or "Jesus calls out hypocrisy"? The way this story has been labeled has directed us to cast guilt on the woman for the alleged adultery and to ignore her humanity. It also contributes to blaming women for sexual promiscuity, in general, and to blaming prostitutes for their job, which would not exist without clients. What a tragedy.

I do not deny that adultery is condemned throughout the Bible. It clearly is. But the focus of this condemnation is on violation of men's property rights over women, and specifically on the sex act, and not the relational and emotional "cheating" that is actually the problem by today's standards. The Bible makes sex the definition of marriage, and thus the definition of adultery as well.

It should be noted that there are also a whole slew of commands in Leviticus 18 telling the men which women in their lives they cannot have sex with, and the list looks like all the women he would see at a family reunion. This does seem to be good practice, not only for genetic reasons, but it also keeps family dynamics a bit more healthy. In addition, there are a few references condemning bestiality (Lev. 20:15-16). Again, another safe call. In short, a man was allowed to have sex with the women who belonged to him, whether as his wives, concubines, or slaves. We never see comments about what was "allowed" for women on this topic. All the commands are directed toward men and with their interests in mind, as we ought to expect at the time. This reality ought to raise a question for us regarding to what extent the commands that we find in scripture, related to sexual activity and relationships, will be sufficient for us today.

Regardless of the nature of how men and women related to one another, inside or outside of a marriage, it is clear that sexual encounters approved of and encouraged in the Bible were between a male and a female. The "what" and the "why" that justify this position, however, might actually surprise you!

Homosexual Sex?

In light of the "marriage equality" conversation currently afoot around the world today, people often want to know what the Bible "says" about same-sex relationships. Since there was no specific term at that time for such relationships, we cannot expect the Bible to ever address it as such. Note that nothing even remotely related to the topic of homosexuality is attributed to Jesus in the four Gospels. But since saying, "It says nothing," is a bit of a letdown, expanding this conversation to include some of the stories related to this topic can be quite eye-opening.

For starters, we can say that all the commands in scripture are based on an assumption that "approved of" sexual encounters will be heterosexual. That is how they are discussed, and the end result of producing children is usually a part of the conversation. The two commands in the entire Hebrew Bible that denounce a "man lying with a man as he does with a woman" ought to be read and understood in light of the need to grow as a nation (Lev. 18:22; 20:13). There is also one specific Newer Testament reference that condemns what we call gay sexual relations. Notice I said "*sexual relations*" and not *relationships*, thus the issue is clearly about the sex act. To be clear, scripture gives no explicit recognition of mutually loving sexual relationships between two men or two women. But this should not surprise us, since it does not discuss heterosexual marriages as being mutually agreed on, loving, and supportive either.

On to some of the related stories, then. Even though King David is married to five or six women at the same time, his relationship with Jonathan goes on for years and is quite complex. I am not so naïve as to say that David and Jonathan definitely had a sexual relationship. It is quite reasonable to say that scripture depicts them as solid companions to each other and that is all. At the same time, there are nuances within even the way their story is told that imply an intimacy that goes beyond many a platonic relationship today. If you read through 1 Samuel 18–20, you will see what many today refer to as "soul mate" language and a depth of connection that seems to surpass what David experiences with his wives.

Ruth and Naomi ought to make it to this conversation as well. As with David and Jonathan, there is no direct indication of anything sexual between these two women, and they are initially related to one another as mother- and daughter-in-law. When Naomi tells her two daughters-in-law to return home in order to remarry, Ruth "clings" to her legs as it says a man will "cling" to his woman in Genesis 2:24. Maybe this word choice was just for dramatic effect. But what does it say to you that a litany of promises Ruth gives Naomi, found in Ruth 1:16–17, are also used in wedding ceremonies today? "Where you go I will go, and where you stay I will stay. Your people will be my people and your god my god. Where you die I will die, and there I will be buried." At the end of the story, women in the community comment on Ruth's importance to Naomi, saying that Ruth is worth more than seven sons to her! In a culture where sons mean infinitely more than daughters do to a mother, how are we to hear this claim?

For those of you willing to at least consider the possibility, I would also direct you to the letter of Philemon in the Newer Testament. This suggestion can be quite difficult for people to consider, since it involves an intriguing dynamic between Paul and Philemon.

As you read through this short letter (only twenty-five verses), you might notice that Paul is never entirely clear about what it is he would like Philemon to do, and that he uses somewhat manipulative language (vv. 8–9, 14, 19–21), but those are matters for another day. Keep in mind also that the slave's name, Onesimus, means "useful," and that slaves have always been used for both labor and sex. You will note that in verse 11, Paul comments on how Onesimus is now "useful" to both Philemon and Paul. Perhaps this usefulness is only a reference to Onesimus helping Paul while he was imprisoned. Then Paul says that he sends Onesimus, "that is, [his] own heart," back to Philemon (v. 12). In verse 13, Paul indicates that he would prefer to keep Onesimus with him so that "he could be of service" in Philemon's place. In verse 17, Paul says, "If you consider me your partner, welcome him as you would welcome me." I do not mean to read our modern meaning of romantic partner onto this letter, but nowhere else does Paul use this term, "partner" (Greek: koinōnon), and there is an intimacy implied throughout this short letter. Incidentally, koinōnon is used, outside of the canon, to refer to intimate relationships between a man and woman.

You might not see these passages as implying that Paul and Philemon had a sexual or romantic relationship and that Onesimus became "useful" as a go-between for them along those lines. That is fine. But more than one student has asked, without any prompting from me, why Paul would be so down on sex between men (in Rom. 1), given this letter. Especially since this letter has no theological content and no direct commands from Paul in terms of how to handle a situation, it seems to me, at the very least, that this letter was meant to be kept between Paul and Philemon. What do you think?

So let's put these pieces together. There are just a few biblical injunctions against sexual relations between two men. There is no term for a homosexual relationship anywhere in the Bible, though we can see what looks and sounds an awful lot like one a few times, engaged in by rather important people. Since the concern is always focused on the sexual act, and not on the relationship, perhaps we should think about what underlies that concern. What is it about sex between two men (sex between two women is not explicitly addressed) that was so unsettling for the ancient Israelites or for Paul in the Newer Testament? Are their concerns still relevant for us today?

WHAT

Stop and take a bit of an inventory on your own thoughts on this matter. What, exactly, is sex? I'm not talking about anatomy here, but the concept overall. Is it dirty, as in something impure, or is it a natural part of being a human and therefore a good thing? For some people, it is an interesting combination of both: a normal part of human functions, but dirty, and thus it ought to be handled as such.

Furthermore, what do people mean when they refer to "natural" vs. "unnatural" on this topic? Are they referring to the plumbing a person has, and thus the most "natural" way things fit together and lead to procreation, or are they talking about the ways a person wants to experience sex as being natural to them?

When it comes to the voices within scripture, does it matter who we listen to on this topic? For instance, do we listen to Solomon, who is reported to have had hundreds of wives and concubines combined? Then there is Paul, who was proud of being celibate. Jesus speaks not at all about sex, directly, though he does speak about being or becoming a eunuch. Were you aware that three of the most prominent men in the Bible held such divergent views on sex?

Pure or Impure?

It might surprise you to learn that there is very little in the Bible that directly addresses how one ought to view sex. There is no passage in which God says from heaven, "Okay, this sex bit . . . I just gave that to you for the sole purpose of procreation!" But to hear some people discuss "biblical ideas" about sex, you would think that there is such a passage.

What is in scripture that comes closest to discussing sex as a thing, not just as a man "going in" to a woman or men "knowing" their wives, is found in the Song of Solomon (also called "Song of Songs"). Yes, this book is attributed to the man of many wives, perhaps because he might have had some insight into the pleasurable aspects of sex. Interestingly enough, this book was almost cut from the Bible because it lacks any theological content. Its inclusion in the canon was an embarrassment to many early Church Fathers, to the point where they interpreted it as if it is actually a love story between Jesus Christ and the Church, or between God and his people.

I encourage you to read it and imagine two lovers trying to connect one night, like Maria and Tony from "West Side Story," and see what you think. These two are not married, since they are living in two different houses, but they clearly know each other's bodies well and know how the other responds to physical intimacy. This seems to suggest that at least some people at the time saw sex as intended for something beyond just making babies.

It is also quite telling that some men of the early Church were more comfortable talking about sexual intimacy between Christ and the Church or between God and his people than between two humans. First of all, how in the world does that work?! Second, consider how people's views on sex would be influenced by this skewed avoidance of honest conversation about sex.

There is no passage in the Bible where God says that sex is dirty or nasty. There are no passages that claim that sex itself is impure. In fact, given the affirmation of it in Genesis 1–2, one could argue that God is cool with sex.

There are passages in Leviticus that discuss ritual impurity, which means there are things that make people symbolically impure (Lev. 5–15). It is not the act or body part involved that makes a person unclean; it is the bodily discharge that seems to matter. There are also passages that discuss how terrible prostitution or "whoredom" is, but again, it seems that it is not the sex act that is the issue, but that a woman is giving herself to lots of men-not-her-husband.

So where does anyone get the idea that sex is "nasty" or "dirty"?

I suppose we cannot know the origin of this perspective entirely. What we do know is that Paul's comments about sex in 1 Corinthians 7 seem to imply that it is better to avoid sex, if possible. The Church has taken up this command of Paul's when it has required clergy to be abstinent. It is also clear that some of the men in the early Church made a connection between sex and sinfulness, building on one another's thoughts about Genesis 2–3 and various passages in Paul's letters about sin (see chap. 3).

Take a moment to think about this. Even though the Bible gives us no reason to claim that sex is impure, sex and sin were intertwined for some men of the early Church. They have, at the very least, contributed to the current idea of sex being something "dirty." What does that do to people's psyches, given how biologically normal it is to have sexual desires and urges? I don't know about you, but I would be fine if we severed this tie, once and for all.

Natural vs. Unnatural

Paul's comments in Romans 1:26–28 are the main source of the "natural" vs. "unnatural" debate. Many people tend to think that *natural* refers to sex that could lead to procreation and *unnatural* refers to any encounter they would label "perverse," such as pedophilia or bestiality. Paul's use of "natural," however, is concerned with what was acceptable or customary in his culture.

Compare this, for instance, with comments in 1 Corinthians 11:14 regarding hair length, which claim that "nature" teaches us that men are to have short hair. Obviously, haircuts are required to keep this in check. Thus *natural* refers to practices Paul was familiar with, or assumed cultural standards, not anything to do with natural physiology or natural desires.

Thus, "unnatural" sexual expressions are those that fall outside of what Paul knows of as a regular practice. If you would like to equate this idea of *unnatural* with perversity, you still run into issues. *Perversity* is any behavior that someone deems to be wrong or different. Practices such as bestiality and pedophilia-inspired behaviors certainly qualify, since they are abusive expressions of power over non-consenting beings. But beyond that, Paul's definition of *unnatural* seems to be things he personally finds abnormal, and we can be reminded that just because you are not interested in something does not automatically make it wrong.

In the case of Romans 1, it seems that Paul was reacting to sexual practices in temple settings, where men had sex with each other and women took on "unnatural" roles in the sexual encounter. Whatever the case, I suggest that you "judge" Paul's claims on the customary/non-customary level. In other words, regardless of the practice that he was denouncing, he was doing so because it was not acceptable culturally for him. This does lead us to the next section, where we look at the "Why?" of sex.

WHY

While this question of "Why did people have sex?" might also seem rather obvious to us today, the way the Bible discusses it is much less interesting and more limited than most people realize, and for that reason it is well worth your consideration. First, take stock of your own thoughts about why people have sex, before reading further. Is it just for procreation? Is it a gift to humans or a requirement of them? For instance, is it okay for a couple to have sex as a stress release or purely for the fun of it? Or does it always need to be experienced for the sake of leading to procreation?

Procreation?

One of the very first commands in the Hebrew Bible to humans is to "be fruitful and multiply; fill the earth and subdue it" (Gen. 1:28). There is no getting around this fact. But if all we do is read this one line and then turn to each other and say, "See? Sex is for procreation!" then we miss a great deal of the contextual importance of this line: who wrote this and to whom it was written. It is also just the first allusion to sex in the Bible, not the entirety of it.

One of the three promises Yahweh (another name for God) gave Abraham (Gen. 12) was that his descendants would outnumber the stars in the sky or the sands on the seashore. Fulfilling this promise takes making a lot of babies. I suggest that we see Genesis 1:28 in light of this command: "Go! Do your part to make that promise come true!"

This perspective, a focus on procreation as the reason for sex, is affirmed in various ways in the Hebrew Bible. One of the striking examples is the story about Onan, found in Genesis 38: 6–10. It is short, and not-so-sweet, so please do go read it. For our purposes, the issue to note is that in the levirate marriage tradition, Onan was supposed to have sex with his older brother's widow in order to produce offspring in his brother's name. The story tells us that Onan did not want his offspring to have his brother's name, so he pulled out prior to ejaculation. The LORD killed Onan on the spot for this choice: wasting his "seed."

Instead of discussing how realistic you think this scenario is, let's focus on how this story functions as a myth. Onan's role in this story is to serve as an example of what not to do: do not waste your "seed"! Wasting your semen cannot lead to procreation, and for a group of people needing to grow in numbers, this wastefulness cannot be tolerated.

Over the centuries, men within the Church have focused on various nuances of this story. Most interesting, to me, is when they read this story as indicating that God thinks that masturbation (a.k.a. onanism) is wrong. If you or someone you know is of this mind-set, you can rest assured that this passage has been part of creating this idea. The fact that we now scientifically know that "there is plenty more where that came from" does make this misreading of Onan's story all the more tragic.

It is also worth noting that we do not need to continue to "be fruitful and multiply." We have an overpopulation issue today. We currently do not feed everyone adequately. Millions of people live in less than adequate housing, without access to daily resources that many people in the developed world take for granted. "Be fruitful and multiply" made a great deal of sense for the people to whom it was written, but it no longer applies to any group of people today. We absolutely must consult other sources of wisdom and experience beyond the Bible for sound advice on this issue.

There are other reasons that the focus on procreation as the reason for sex can be harmful for people. Some couples choose not to have children or cannot. Are they supposed to abstain from sex? Should the men in these couples expect to be struck down by God for wasting their seed? Plenty of couples enjoy sex for decades after the female reaches menopause. Is this a misuse of a gift?

Perhaps my questions sound silly, but they are the logical conclusions one can draw from saying that sex is only for the sake of procreation. There is no denying that the perpetuation of the human species depends on men and women having sex. But to say that is the only reason for sex is also incredibly limiting.

This argument, that sex is only about procreation, significantly undergirds the perspective that marriage should be only between a man and a woman. If you remove the "that-act-is-meant-to-create-a-baby" idea, you can focus on two people in love. If a person is no longer thinking that procreation must be a possibility for a sex act to be "right," then the judgment directed toward gays and lesbians for the ways they enjoy intimacy no longer holds water.

The primary, procreative reason for sex in the biblical context is not the only reason for us today. These are not light or insignificant matters. The "why" of sex is actually the most important aspect of it for us to wrestle with in order to apply biblical passages in a way that leads to love instead of judgment, guilt, or animosity. Permission granted.

Because It Is Fun?

Please let the record show that I am a big proponent of always respecting and honoring yourself in this arena and being safe and responsible.

That said, many Christians I know have been done a disservice because their faith tradition has taught them about sex in such a controlled and sanitized way that the pleasure of it is difficult to get to.

As I mentioned above, there is one book in the Bible that suggests to us that sex can be pleasurable, and that is Song of Solomon (Song of Songs). Unfortunately, there is only one book that does this. It is not likely to be read in a worship context or as the focus of a Bible study, thus many Christians are unaware of its existence (unless they are taught the spiritualized version that reads it as the love between Christ and the Church). So, if we have to stick with what the Bible does say about sex, we have come to the end of the matter.

But there is one final topic I would like to discuss in this chapter: rape in the Bible. Let me be clear: rape is not sex. These are two very different things. I have chosen to include it in this chapter instead of the one on violence, however, because of how some of the passages involved are often misread as being about sex.

RAPE IN THE BIBLE

First, some people are surprised to hear that rape is even talked about in the Bible. This response is understandable, since their perception of what this holy book contains may have been limited to what they heard in worship settings in the past.

But more important, we need to be clear that in spite of sex and rape looking somewhat similar from a certain perspective, they are not at all the same. Sex is mutually entered into. Rape is forced. Sex is at least intended to be mutually enjoyable. Rape is unsolicited and unwelcomed. Rape is an act of power and dominance by one person over another and is done specifically with the intent to harm or shame. The memory, trauma, and physicality of rape leave emotional scars that do not ever fully heal.

This topic applies to the story about Sodom and Gomorrah. Yes, the act those men wanted to "perform" was rape, not sex. That means that the "issue" being addressed in that passage was not homosexuality but cruelty. There are also a few stories where women are raped, but no one in the story seems terribly upset about it for the reasons we might be today. See what you think.

Sodom and Gomorrah

A discussion of Sodom and Gomorrah properly belongs in this section about rape, not within the context of homosexual intercourse. If you are already confused or sensing your defenses going up, please take a moment to read the story for yourself with a few contextual prompts. The story that people usually focus on is found in Genesis 19, but the story of Sodom begins in chapter 18. The LORD and Abraham have a discussion about the people of Sodom, and the LORD says that he would like to destroy the entire town due to its wickedness. Righteousness or wickedness were defined, in large part, by the way people treated one another.

As you read Genesis 19:1–11, consider these questions: Why do you think it was so important to Lot to invite the two men into his home? What music would you put in the background of verses 4–9, if you were filming this scene?

As you thoughtfully read Genesis 19:1–11, I hope it became clear that it was important to Lot to welcome strangers, whether due to his own code of being kind to strangers or because he knew how cruel the people of Sodom could be. When people discuss what the background music should be when all the men of Sodom come and surround the house, they consistently suggest something appropriate for a scary scene. None of these men were in an amorous mood; they had cruelty on their minds.

You may be aware that, within the Bible, wanting "to know" someone is a euphemism for "have sex with." But that does not mean that what is intended here is sex. The men say they want to know the two visitors; but what they wish to do is rape the guests who are in Lot's house—an act of violence intended to punish the visitors for being in their town. It may be that lines such as this one in the Bible, that confuse sex with rape, contribute significantly to the way some people mistake them for the same thing today.

This whole scene is deeply disturbing to me every time I read it. First, these men who were strangers to Lot are of more value or worth to him than his own daughters. Culturally speaking, it would have been a greater disgrace to allow the rape of those two men than of his own two daughters. Second, Lot acknowledges that virgin women are literally more valuable than women who are not. These social realities, spoken by Lot, seem to cross his lips so easily and naturally. So much meaning for such a short sentence. Finally, 19:9 suggests that the men of the town are fully aware that they were going to be cruel to these two visitors.

In short, there is nothing consensual or loving about the kind of interaction that would have taken place, had the angels not blinded all the men of the town. It was raping, shaming, and being cruel that was on the minds of the men of Sodom, whether the visitors happened to be male or female. This story has nothing to do with homosexual intercourse. It has everything to do with Yahweh condemning cruel and inhospitable actions. Genesis 19 is intended to send a message about how important it was for the people of Israel to be welcoming to strangers.

You should know that people can hear this interpretation of the story and still maintain that the issue is homosexuality. While this also disturbs me deeply, I do understand their response. They have been told for so long that Sodom was doomed because of homosexuality that one alternate reading is not enough to change their mind about it. After all, the terms *sodomy* and *sodomize* come from this passage, indicating how deeply ingrained one particular view of this passage is.

But this resistance to seeing the Sodom and Gomorrah story as about hospitality nonetheless disturbs me. First, it means that this person is equating rape with consensual sex. It terrifies me that sexually active people can confuse the two. Second, it highlights the complicated relationship between people's faith and what they see in the Bible. It says something that a person can find a way to embrace the idea that the message of this passage is that "God hates homosexuals" but resist a more loving interpretation: "God hates cruelty." The irony is that, in embracing the animosity that comes from the first interpretation, a person is often guilty of the real "sin of Sodom": being inhospitable and cruel.

Other Stories Containing Rape

We need to be clear that just because something is in the Bible does not mean that God condones it. There are some things that are narrated specifically to warn people how not to behave. So just because someone gets raped in the Bible does not mean that it is just fine with God. The trouble here is that it is not always clear that God is upset about this horrific treatment of women. In one case in particular, it seems God is actually in agreement with it, since it is part of a message that God is sending through the prophet Hosea (chap. 5). So, instead of telling you what the

Bible says in these stories, I will direct you to them and give you some suggestions for considering them in context. The primary stories that I would direct you to are about Dinah (Gen. 34), an unnamed concubine (Jdg. 19), and one of David's daughters, Tamar (2 Sam. 13).

Dinah's story is often referred to as "the rape of Dinah" even though, according to the story, Shechem raped Dinah then immediately fell in love with her. I assure you that this is highly unlikely to happen in real life. He either raped her or he loved her; not both. You also might want to think about Dinah's voice in this story (whether or not you read and liked Anita Diamant's novel *The Red Tent*) and what it is you think this story was told to justify.

Judges 19–20 discusses a Levite and his concubine and the subsequent war that breaks out because of how they are treated by members of another tribe of Israel. This story has striking resemblances to the story of Sodom and has a similar takeaway: be hospitable to one another! But the way this unnamed concubine is treated throughout the story by the Levite and how she ends up being gang raped all night do not sit well with many people.

The story of David's daughter Tamar is particularly interesting, since we get to see three men's reaction to her half-brother Amnon raping her. Whatever the reason for the story, please note what happens to Tamar and how David and Absolom, Tamar's oldest brother, respond. I am afraid that David does not come out looking as courageous as he does in other stories (see also chap. 6), the David who is labeled "a man after God's heart."

In addition to these three examples of women being raped or used as examples in such ways, there are other stories, some quite central to the overall biblical narrative, in which the women involved have no choice in the copulative act. Does this make it rape? Hagar, in Genesis 16, has no choice in being "given" to Abraham so that he may "go into her," and have a child with her. In Genesis 12, Sarah is taken into the Pharaoh's concubinage in order that things may go well for Abraham. This sounds rather like Abraham is pimping out Sarah to save himself, and it works! But at what cost to Sarah? Many people read David's first encounter with Bathsheba as a rape, since she had no choice in the matter.

Rape and sexual assault are serious matters. The trauma they inflict on people's psyches and souls, not to mention bodies, takes away a part of them that is usually never fully restored. The fact that there are depictions of rape scenes in the Bible, where the victims' realities are swept under the carpet, ought to give you something to think about. Permission granted.

CONCLUSION

Perhaps it is okay to say that sex is beautiful and complex and delightful and that it is a natural thing to desire. Desires are a natural part of being human instead of impure and shameful, as many of us have been told. And those who are concerned about sex's connection to procreation should remind themselves of the global population count and be thankful that some sexually active people are not adding to the numbers. Allow me to suggest, once again, that we need to turn to resources beyond the Bible for guidance on determining what healthy sex is and looks like today.

 TAKE THE BIBLE INTO YOUR OWN HANDS

1. What is your definition of "biblical marriage"? In light of modern ideas about women and marriage, how should we think about the wide range of models of marriage in the Bible?

2. What is your response to the idea that the Bible focuses on the sex act as defining marriage? Is this the way marriage is defined for you?

3. Which messages about sex that we see in the Bible do you want children today to learn and embrace? Are there healthy ideas about sex that are not represented in the Bible that you think should also be a part of this conversation?

4. Given the Bible's focus on the sex act, and procreation specifically, how should we engage the ideas about marriage in a productive conversation about same-sex marriages today? Do we need to continue to uphold the ability to procreate as central to a marriage, for instance?

5. How do you handle passages in the Bible that narrate a rape? What do you think about examples that we interpret to seem less violent and offensive than they really are (such as Sodom) or that no one in the story (including God) seems to disapprove of?

5

Violence: The Language Everyone Understands

One of the most difficult things to point out to people is how much violence there is in the Bible. Of course, just because there is violence depicted in the Bible does not mean that it is something that God approves of, and this is an important distinction to make. But the passages I am inviting you to read and to think about in this chapter are all related to commands that come from God or that depict something violent that the author implies that God is okay with. There are parts of this chapter that will invite you to think about the worldview underlying the scriptures, and other parts will focus on practices or world views that make their way into common interpretations of scripture. My motivation is to invite you to take an honest look at what is going on in these passages and to take a few moments to think about their implications.

First, spend some time taking stock of your view of violence in general. For instance, is it ever called for? Is violence in response to an injustice different than violence as a result of losing one's patience? Why do people use violence? Does the level of intimacy affect things? What about the use of angry words or bullying? Where does emotional or relational violence fit into this picture?

There are two main reasons for taking stock in this way. The first is to highlight the numerous realms of our lives in which violence happens. The second is to get you thinking about what violent behaviors say about the person doing them. Apply these thoughts to what we see in the Bible and you may find yourself wondering about the men who wrote these stories, and to what degree their worldview is helpful for us today.

Passages in this chapter involve battle imagery, consequences carried out by God (who is also referred to as Yahweh or the LORD), the sacrificial system, the commands to kill people for certain violations, passages that depict abuse or careless treatment of people, and passages that use violent or manipulative language. Some of this may be a matter of how you read the passages, in which case we might see them differently. Nonetheless, I hope you will give them an honest, open reading.

Battle Imagery

This first category is perhaps the most obvious one. It is stunning not just how often battles are depicted but also how many times God endorses murdering other people. At times God fights on behalf of the Israelites. All of this suggests that God is fine with the use of violence and killing for the benefit of God's people. It is perhaps most disturbing in Joshua, as Joshua is promised that God will deliver one group of people after another into the Israelites' hands. Time after time, the Israelites are said to have "devoted to destruction" all the inhabitants of a town, because this is what God told them to do. I encourage you to read Joshua 6–11 for the larger context of these excerpts:

> The city and all that is in it shall be devoted to the LORD for destruction. (6:17)

> Then the LORD said to Joshua, "Stretch out the sword that is in your hand toward Ai; for I will give it into your hand." (8:18)

> The total of those who fell that day, both men and women, was twelve thousand—all the people of Ai. (8:25)

> "[P]ursue your enemies, and attack them from the rear. Do not let them enter their towns, for the LORD your God has given them into your hand." (10:19)

> Joshua took Makkedah on that day, and struck it and its king with the edge of the sword; he utterly destroyed every person in it; he left no one remaining. . . . The LORD gave [Libnah] also and its king

into the hand of Israel; and he struck it with the edge of the sword, and every person in it; he left no one remaining in it. (10:28–30)

So Joshua defeated the whole land . . . he left no one remaining, but utterly destroyed all that breathed, as the LORD God of Israel commanded. (10:40)

Joshua did to them as the LORD commanded him; he hamstrung their horses, and burned their chariots with fire. (11:9)

I think you get the idea. As passages such as Joshua 8:25 and 10:28 indicate, utterly destroying every person in a town included the women and children and not simply the warriors in battle. It is also somewhat curious that in addition to God siding with Israel in their battles against enemies, as in these examples, God also sides with some of the tribes of Israel against the others, after they had split into two kingdoms. Hmmm.

Battle imagery is used to speak about the spiritual realm, as well. Before the Israelites begin to conquer Canaan, Joshua has a vision of an angel standing before him with a sword in his hand, claiming to be the commander of the army of the LORD. Similarly, this idea is used sporadically throughout the Newer Testament and in a fairly concentrated way in Ephesians 6:10–17, which describes the "armor of God."

As the Ephesians 6 passage indicates, this is not just a Hebrew Bible issue. Many times people want to say that the God of the Hebrew Bible is violent and the God of the Newer Testament is all-loving. This is, quite simply, not the case. God is described both ways in both testaments. There are numerous examples of the God of the Hebrew Bible as abounding in steadfast love, merciful and gracious (Exod. 34:6). On the flip side, in addition to the "armor of God," the word of God is compared with a sword several times in the Newer Testament, and in Revelation, it figuratively wounds and murders some people. Some things that Jesus says in John's Gospel are hateful and angry beyond a righteous anger (8:39-47). As someone speaking on God's authority and about God's son, Paul has moments of judgmental anger or frustration in his letters (Gal. 1; Rom. 1) and speaks of the life of faith in battle terms on several occasions (Phil. 1:27–30; 1 Tim. 1:18).

While I do understand that the battle imagery works well, I am not sure how beneficial it is to think of God as a warrior and God's children as soldiers. Having God "on your side" is a pretty powerful concept. It

Soldiers for the LORD

What does it do to a person's worldview to talk about reality, or faith, using battle metaphors? Just because they are prevalent and powerful does not mean that they are beneficial. They are applied in various contexts, such as, "I'm a soldier in the army of the Lord," or "I'm a prayer warrior." Ephesians 6, and its discussion of the armor of God, highlights the idea that life is a battle.

How do people tend to apply the terms "soldier of Christ" or "the Lord's army" in our culture today? In my online search of the first phrase I came across all kinds of Sunday school and Vacation Bible School (VBS) curricula playing off of this theme. I saw "Bible Boot Camp" or resources for army-themed VBS material, geared specifically toward children. The site describing "B.O.O.T. camp: Biblical Outlook and Outreach Training" includes gift bags with "Soldier of God" camouflage bookmarks, camouflage rubber silicone bracelets, and "Soldier of God" temporary tattoos.

Red flags go up when I see "army" and "children" in the same sentence, and not just because of the children's armies of the past few decades in Africa. The "us vs. them" mentality behind battle metaphors and language concerns me. Children will be deeply influenced by the mentality they are taught to have: one that creates spaces of love, support, and inclusion, or one that sees the world as a battlefield for God/Christ.

Consider the thoughts of Bishop Steven Charleston, the former president and dean of the Episcopal Divinity School, from in one of his online posts: "The spiritual life is not a struggle. Even when it confronts the greatest trials of our time . . . it is not a power that requires the exercise of force. . . . It is in trust that confidence arises."

has granted some the conviction that any action can be justified if it is done for God's glory.

EXTREME PUNISHMENTS

In this section, I am suggesting that the motives attributed to God or God's reactions at times are worth holding up for inspection. When the things depicted in scripture do not fit with a God of love, compassion, and forgiveness, then it seems fair to me to say that they did not come from such a God. The form or extreme nature of the punishment in some of the stories is also worth assessing.

The Premise behind the Flood Stories (Gen. 6–10)

The reason given for the flood happening is based on God being sorry for creating humans. If you are of a mind to take scripture at face value, instead of looking for the mythic part of it, then you believe that God was really sorry for creating humans, and so God killed all but one family of them in order to start all over.

Reading this story in a literal way, you are left worshiping an impetuous God, who is somewhat lacking in creativity in the problem-solving department. There are people who believe that God is truly not just capable of, but willing to do this. They worship a God they literally fear and find a way to also love this God, because they believe that God could do the same thing again today. As any mental health professional will tell you, the combination of fearing but feeling compelled to love someone else is foundational to an abusive relationship.

Reading these stories as myths, however, allows us to see that the authors of these stories needed to give some reason for the terrible fact of recurrent flooding, and perhaps playfully to explain why rainbows occur. The authors choose to use these natural phenomena to promote these two distinct promises given in Genesis 8:22 and 9:15. The seasons will continue in their courses, and the whole earth will never again be flooded. The fact that flooding continues in various places around the world anyway is not a signal that God broke a promise. It is just a reality of what happens with heavy rains and overflowing rivers. When read literally, God is a promise-breaker and is sorry for creating humanity. Reading the flood stories as myths gives us insight into what natural phenomena the people needed explanations for.

Exodus 32

Many people know of the "golden calf" story, which is found at the beginning of Exodus 32. For the sake of context, I hope you will read the entire chapter. Here, I would like to focus on what happens at the end, in Exodus 32:25–29.

Reading this passage out loud makes the horrific nature of the scene a bit more real, so I hope you might do that. Either way, what does it say to you that Moses stands before the people of Israel and commands those brave enough to take up their swords and kill their brothers, friends, and neighbors (32:27)? Not only that, but the men who do so are commended for it and are given the important role of being priests for the LORD.

The mythic value of the story is that, given Aaron's mistake regarding the statue, a new tribe, those who proved themselves appropriately zealous for the LORD, will be priests. But myth or not, this passage is dripping in blood spilled by the hands of family members. Isn't it a relief to be able to say that these aspects might be the desires of the humans who wrote the story and not those of God?

Leviticus 26

The book of Leviticus is intended to show the people how they can remain pure and holy in order to be pleasing in God's sight. Chapter 26 begins by describing the rewards for those who are obedient, and they are amazing promises. If the people of Israel will worship only Yahweh, then Yahweh promises to give them rain when they need it for plentiful crops, peace in the land, and safety from wild animals and their enemies. In short, everything they need!

If they are not obedient, however, God will handle the people in quite the opposite way. Please read Leviticus 26:14–33. God promises to bring terror on such people and will allow their enemies to defeat them. Their fields will produce nothing, and wild animals will overtake them. "I will continue hostile to you in fury; I in turn will punish you myself sevenfold for your sins" (v. 28). Even mobsters do not make threats of this level of retaliation. This passage, and many others in the Hebrew Bible, uses fear to elicit submission. Is that the true nature of God, or just a tactic attributed to God by the writers?

Achan's Punishment

The story of Achan and his family comes at the beginning of the Israelites' conquering of Canaan (Josh. 7) and sends a clear message about how the Israelites are to handle all the goods they would procure as they slaughter town after town of people. When it comes to the things that are to be devoted to God, people are not to keep any of it for themselves. Period. Achan ignores this command (given in Josh. 6:18–21), and this angers the LORD greatly. I encourage you to read Joshua 7 with some curiosity, paying attention to the details of the story and the way Achan's family is singled out. In the end, Achan and his family are taken, stoned, and then burned.

I do not question the need to "teach a lesson." What I would encourage you to think about is the extreme nature of the punishment. It is not only a matter of whether or not the crime merits such a consequence. It is also a matter of what this tells us about the people writing the story. It is noteworthy that they think the threat of such extreme consequences is necessary to keep people in line. Additionally, do you really want to worship a God who threatens to interact with people by such extreme measures? (I truly hope not.)

Ananias and Sapphira

The story about Ananias and Sapphira is in Acts 5:1–11. It comes immediately after a passage in Acts that tells how all of Jesus' followers in Jerusalem took care of one another by sharing all their belongings with the members of their community (Acts 4:34–35).

Ananias and Sapphira are a couple who choose not to share with the community the proceeds from the sale of some land. When confronted, they both lie about it and both die on the spot because of their deception. Their story is another one of those "what not to do" examples. And as in the story of Achan, it seems to me to use rather extreme consequences. If we want to teach people not to lie and not to be greedy, there must be a better way to do it than with the threat of death. Keep in mind that children's imaginations allow them to believe that such dying-on-the-spot consequences are truly possible today. The common justification for these violent stories, that "God's ways are higher than our own," does nothing to mitigate a child's fear that God might smite him or her in that same way.

Conclusion to Punishments

For now, I would encourage you to weigh in on whether or not the motives attributed to God in these stories line up with who you believe

God is. In terms of the extreme punishments for disobedience that are depicted in these and other stories, do consider whether these are tactics you think are beneficial for people today.

Let me be clear. It concerns me to see such extreme punishments attributed to God and not questioned by people today. Whether the story writers believed that God was able to zap people dead, on the spot, or thought that it was just an effective way to make a point, think of what such violence and extreme measures will do to a belief system or view of the world.

SACRIFICIAL SYSTEM

One of the reasons this topic can be so difficult for some people to see afresh is because it is intimately connected to the main way Christians make sense of Jesus' crucifixion. But it is because of this connection that I think it is important to think about the system of sacrifices and offerings in the Hebrew Bible, in terms of what it was accomplishing and why it "worked." Starting there, then looking to the crucifixion, can be quite eye-opening.

Leviticus has the explanation of offerings and sacrificing of animals. As you read the first chapter of Leviticus, note that verses 3 and 4 highlight part of why this system works. The animal stands in on the person's behalf. The death of this animal allows for atonement between the person and the LORD. "What is atonement?" you might ask. The easy way to explain it is to pull the word apart: creating at-one-ment between two people or groups who have fallen out of relationship.

Think about what is going on here. This sacrificial system is based on the idea that when humans sin they offend God so deeply that they deserve to die for their error or behavior. Humans just being human make God that angry. The "solution," the way to appease God's anger, is to take a life. In doing so, people show how much they wish to be back in good standing with God. Now, I am not challenging the idea that this animal, in needing to be without blemish and having come from someone's own flock, is important to the person. I am trying to push you to consider two things: humans' sins might not offend God to the extent this system claims, and there might be a way of creating at-one-ment without taking a life.

Next, there is the part about what the priests do with the carcass, and the blood in particular. Leviticus 1:5 tells us that the priests were to dash the blood of the bull "against all sides of the altar that is at the entrance of the tent of meeting." Can you picture this scene? Think about how much blood there would be, splattered all over an altar.

The scent in the air is another element of the picture, certainly. The whole body of the animal was laid on the firewood. The reason for this is because burning the flesh creates a "pleasing odor to the LORD" (Lev. 1:9b). Pleasing odor. This is part of the understanding behind why animal sacrifices "worked." As a former meat-eater, I can confirm that grilling meat smells divine for many people. The writers of Leviticus seemed to think that God enjoys the scent of a barbeque as well.

To be clear, there were also other kinds of offerings, such as grain offerings and offerings of well-being and sin offerings, some also accomplished through the killing of an animal. Countless students have asked me over the years, "Why are they picking on/killing the animals so much?" But the question highlights the point. It is important to grasp that it did make sense to the people at the time to kill an animal as a way to appease God. It is also worth keeping in mind that this way of viewing the human/deity relationship is found in ancient traditions around the world, and that at times humans were also sacrificed.

The animal sacrificial system did come to an end long ago, not just for Christians but for Jews as well, but the central idea of taking a life in order to "make things right" between God and the people of God continues in some faith communities to this day. Based on the premise behind the sacrificial system, many Christians believe that human sinfulness not only angers God but also deserves the punishment of death and that Jesus was killed as a substitute for us. In this sense, people view Jesus as taking the role of the sacrificial animals talked about in Leviticus. This interpretation of Jesus' death is referred to as "substitutionary atonement," for obvious reasons.

The premise behind the sacrificial system was that humans being human angered God to such a degree that the relationship was severed. The offerings and sacrifices were thought to appease God's anger. Notice there are no commands to go and ask forgiveness of the people in your life you might have offended or wronged. The focus is on pleasing the deity, which is a concern that runs throughout many ancient peoples' belief systems. I hope you will think about whether all of that squares with the way you see God and humans today.

THE DEATH PENALTY

One major question on the topic of violence in the Bible is this fascinating contradiction we find in the Laws and commandments regarding murder. Number six of the "Ten Commandments" tells us not to
murder. It seems pretty simple. Yet the LORD also tells the Israelites to
put people to death as a consequence for more than just one or two
offenses described in the other commandments. So which is it?

For starters, there are quite a few Hebrew words that refer to some
form of homicide in the Hebrew Bible. You can compare this to all the
terms we have for killing someone, in light of intention or how violent
it is and so forth. For instance, think of the distinctions embedded
in terms such as *homicide, manslaughter, slaughter,* and *annihilate.* So
it is in the Hebrew Bible. The term used in the sixth commandment
implies premeditation: do not plot to kill one another, essentially.

This explanation does not resolve the issue, however, because there
are still all those commands to put people to death, in response to
sometimes seemingly minor infractions. For some of these examples,
you might want to read through Exodus 20–24. These commands say
to put to death anyone who curses or strikes his or her mother or father.
Worshiping another god, being a female "sorcerer," and kidnapping
were all also deemed worthy of death. Death. (Really?!) By the way,
now you know why the witch hunts led to putting to death the people
found guilty. It is right there in scripture to kill such a person (though
many of the victims were males as well).

Then there are all the eye-for-an-eye and tooth-for-a-tooth kinds
of commands. This kind of punishment set down in law is referred to
as a *lex talionis.* As you can hear in the root of the second word, this is
based on an idea of *retaliation*: you harm or injure someone, the same
harm or injury will be done to you. Perhaps this form of punishment or
retribution makes sense in a primitive setting, but continuing to apply
this rule will make the whole world blind and toothless.

The trouble I have with a repay-in-kind punishment for crimes
is twofold. First, retaliation is rarely, if ever, satisfactory. While it is
something terrible—horrible—when someone loses a child to murder,
putting that murderer to death rarely resolves anything for the family.
Many people who have had a family member murdered will tell you
so. Second, such retaliatory punishments perpetuate a cycle of violence
and aggression and teach people to think this way instead of working

toward forgiveness. It is difficult for me to see how punishing an act of violence with another form of violence serves any of us well.

This is another one of those situations where simply saying that our cultural values on these issues have progressed is not sufficient. Taken as a whole, the attitudes toward discipline or how to handle problems, which are embedded in these scriptures, perpetuate a worldview that is comfortable with violence and force.

PASSAGES THAT SHOW ABUSE
OR CARELESS TREATMENT OF WOMEN

This section addresses some rarely referenced passages from the Hebrew Bible and one rather well-known passage from the Newer Testament. Those that are less well-known tend to surprise people. "Who knew that such a perspective on women was in the Bible?" More familiar passages tend to be difficult to know how to handle. They sound somewhat difficult for women, yet, for those who hold the Bible close, simply dismissing these passages is not an option. As you read through this next section, and the related biblical passages, please do keep your eyes and mind open, looking for these two things: 1) Would you like men today to imitate what we see the men, or God, do in these Hebrew Bible passages? 2) In what ways do you see people applying the messages from the Newer Testament passage today?

Stories in Judges

As you read these two stories, you should know that the judges in Israel were sought as much for wisdom as for their potential to lead the Israelites into battle. Ultimately, the way the stories are told makes it seem that judges were not sufficient for keeping the people of Israel on the straight and narrow. Thus, we might or might not find the judges worth emulating.

Judges 11:29–40. The first story is about Jephthah and his daughter. The back-story summary is that Jephthah was born to a sex worker and for this reason was disowned by his half-brothers. Jephthah, being a bit of a rough character, was later called on by these same people to help them defeat their enemies. He agrees to help only if, in the event that they are victorious, he could be their ruler. Done and done.

The part of the story related to the topic at hand comes in Judges 11:29–40. As you read it, pay attention to the vow to the LORD that Jephthah comes up with: that he will sacrifice the first thing to come through the door on his return home. Since he is a widower, with one daughter, he ought to have been pretty clear who would be involved in this vow. I also cannot help but wonder if he would have been so cavalier had his only child been a son.

There are other fascinating tidbits in this story worth wondering about, such as why the daughter was so willing to die or why it was something worth mourning that she died a virgin. But I hope you will think about the way Jephthah's daughter, never named in the story, is treated and which part of the story is worth emulating. All in all, since God neither condones nor judges what happens, this story is thoroughly unsettling for many people.

Judges 19:15–24. Many of the same questions will likely come to mind in this passage as those that did when you read chapter 11. This woman is also unnamed (again?!). The actions of the man are not condemned by God. And this woman also comes to a fairly gruesome end. I would hope that all these pieces would raise questions for you, especially when you read how the man is reported to have been somewhat responsible for the woman's death.

As you read this story, please think about the following things. First, the woman is called a *concubine*, which means that the man already had at least one wife and was acquiring this woman for sexual engagements. Second, the two primary ways of translating why the concubine left radically change the way you will read the dynamics of the whole story. Was she mad at him, or he at her? Given the way the story plays out, the former seems more likely to me. Think of what it says that he would "speak tenderly to her and bring her back," if he has been cruel or harsh with her, and that the father stalls their departure. If you think about the underlying dynamic implied in this falling-out, you will find that it is quite similar to the dynamics of abusive relationships today.

I am deeply troubled every time I read or talk about this story. I hope you were careful to read through it actively, not passively. Notice how Judges 19:15–24 sounds quite similar to the story in Genesis 19, which addresses a lack of hospitality in Sodom (see chap. 4). The primary difference, however, is that in Judges 19 no one steps in to stop the men of Gibeah from raping the concubine, as the angels did to protect Lot and his company. When confronted with the possibility of being raped himself, the Levite offers his concubine to stand in his place, and she is taken and ravaged all night.

I realize that this is a terrible, horrible scene and that we are not meant to like that the men of the town gang-rape a woman all night long, but why is it okay for both men in the house to think of handing over the women instead, and so easily? The answer is found in the question. Women were not seen as being as valuable as men at that time. Women were property and could be dealt with however a man saw fit. I would like to think that we could all agree that "believing what the Bible says," on this particular topic, is not an option for us today.

Hosea

I distinctly recall a women's weekend retreat, in my college years, for which the first two chapters of Hosea were the focus in one of the Bible studies. The fact that a woman/wife is being used in this passage to make a point made it seemingly appropriate for our context. I do not remember exactly what was said. What I do remember is feeling deeply disturbed, and that I left early because of how uncomfortable I was, though at the time I could not put words to why. It was my first encounter with such a disturbing passage in the Bible being taught as a source of guidance for our lives.

It is helpful for you to understand how the prophets' messages and symbolic actions functioned. The prophets in the Hebrew Bible were responding to matters that were happening in their midst. They offered messages to the people of Israel, speaking in first person, as if they were the LORD talking to them. Most of their messages fall into two distinct categories. The first are warnings, especially to the leadership of Israel, to get back on track with keeping their end of the covenant with the LORD. The other group of messages are words of encouragement and hope, especially during the Israelites' time in exile.

Hosea is one of the Hebrew Bible prophets known for having delivered messages through symbolic actions. This means that the message from God to the people would be embodied in the action of the prophet. For instance, the LORD told Hosea to take "a wife of whoredom" (marry a sex-worker). The LORD was speaking about Israel worshiping other gods as comparable to a wife prostituting herself to many lovers. The message that follows is one of warning to the people to keep the covenant.

Anytime you see content in poetic form, it is an indication that Hosea is saying these things on the LORD's behalf. As you read the first couple of chapters of Hosea, please pay attention to what is described in 2:2–14.

Did you read it? I wonder how you reacted when you saw in 2:2, 4 that God threatens to strip Israel naked and kill her with thirst. The phrase "uncover her shame in the sight of her lovers" means that he will have sex with her in front of others (2:10). This is, at the very least, a form of pornography, given the event will be watched. But it could be interpreted as a rape scene as well, since it sounds like a threat, "and no one shall rescue her from my hand" (2:10).

My stomach goes weak every time I read Hosea 2:14. After figuratively stripping Israel naked and having sex with her in front of an audience, God says that he will allure her to a solitary place and speak tenderly to her. I am sorry to have to point this out, again, but this is precisely the pattern that abusive husbands or partners employ. Let me explain what I mean.

After some form of abuse or violence, which the abuser will typically say was triggered by something the woman did or did not do, the man usually cools down and tries to speak tenderly to the abused woman in order to "win her back." He also usually tries to keep her isolated from others and to scare her into being quiet about it all. I realize that this is quite an extreme, intense scenario that I am suggesting here, but if you were to ask a woman living in a shelter for survivors of domestic violence, I am confident that she or her children would confirm the parallel between their own experience of abuse and what is described in these scriptures.

Perhaps you can see why I was deeply unsettled that day, many years ago. The teacher was oriented toward agreeing with everything in scripture instead of being able to see some of it as abusive. This is another one of the passages that fuels my concern when I hear people say that they "believe the Bible."

I hope that you are not fine with the portrayal of a God who speaks with intimidating threats and whose messages to the people evoke scenes of violence and abuse of women. You don't have to believe that God would do these things. Permission granted.

1 Peter 3:1–6

This passage is near and dear to my heart, having been the focus of my first book. But I will resist going into too much detail and focus specifically on the elements of it that address the treatment of women. Remember, I am hoping that you will think about ways that you see this and similar Newer Testament passages being applied or lived out today.

Read Peter's admonitions in 3:1–6, and perhaps 2:18–25 as well. Think about the parts of a woman's life that are being addressed.

"Accepting a husband's authority" will loom over her every action. There are commands that address the way she dresses and adorns herself. She is told to be quiet and self-controlled. In short, every aspect of a woman's life is affected by this short list of commands, and it is effectively shutting off all self-expression and self-determination.

The reference to Sarah is also quite telling. Consider verse 6, which might be more accurately translated: "You have become [Sarah's] daughters as long as you do what is good and are never frightened by terrifying things." (Compare this verse to the English translation you are using and see how much gentler translators have made it sound!) The only time the scriptures tell us that Sarah endured something terrifying is when she is taken into the concubinage of two different men (Gen. 12 and 20). Those first nights as a concubine have forced sex in the background, which she endured for the sake of her husband. Sarah's story is being used as an example for the women in Asia Minor, who are apparently experiencing frightening things at the hands of their husbands.

Because of this passage, there are well-meaning pastors who advise abused women to stay in a home or relationship. Many abused women are advised to "win over" their abuser with their actions, also because of this passage. The thing is, abusive situations only get worse with time, no matter what the victim says or does. This advice, however well intended, is utterly misguided, because, when applied, it leads to harm for many people. I have heard one scholar redeem this specific passage on behalf of women who, for various economic and political reasons, are truly not able to get out of an abusive situation. I would like to think that we would not choose that as a default, however. What do you think?

Conclusion to Treatment of Women

These and other passages that send their message through the abuse or control of women do not sit well with me, and I hope that they do not with you either. They bring to light part of the worldview of the authors of scripture. They certainly highlight the fact that women were seen as second-class citizens and as property of the men in their lives. Just because parts of scripture embrace violence, force, and the control of women does not mean that it is God's idea, or even a good idea, to perpetuate that treatment of women today.

VIOLENCE, THREATS, AND MANIPULATION IN THE NEWER TESTAMENT

In case you are wondering if all the violence is in the Hebrew Bible, let me assure you that it is not. The Newer Testament is much shorter than the Hebrew Bible, however, and is comprised of different kinds of writings. For many Christians it can be difficult to acknowledge unsettling things along these lines in the Gospels or Paul's letters. But they are there in scripture, so we need to give them a serious look.

Words of Jesus

Many people are taught to read Jesus' parables and words in general as if he is speaking of spiritual matters all the time. One of the most shocking things to learn, then, is that most of Jesus' parables and his interactions with the Jewish leadership are about politics and money, not people's souls.

For instance, Matthew 10:34 records Jesus as having said to his disciples: "Do not think that I have come to bring peace to the earth; I have not come to bring peace, but a sword." This verse inevitably comes up as one of the most confusing, I hope for obvious reasons.

If you view Jesus' actions and words as if he stands in the tradition of the Hebrew Bible prophets, properly understood, you can see that he wants to address financial and political problems (think of Amos as his precursor). These are problems that affect "the masses," the people Jesus is said to have interacted with every day. We know that Jesus was living in a time when the leaders of the Jews were financially exploiting their own people. Maybe Jesus saw the severity of the oppression and exploitation of the people as requiring that he and his followers take up arms to address it. Maybe he knew that his message calling out the leadership would cause others to take up arms. However you make sense of this verse, beware of turning it into an issue that is only playing out spiritually.

There are other examples from Jesus' words you might want to think about. For instance, Matthew 25:31–46 is a story about separating the righteous people from those bound for eternal judgment, comparing them to sheep and goats. If you set aside any notions of justice in this scene—"Everyone is getting what they deserve"—then you might be able to ask yourself about the excessiveness of the punishment Jesus threatens. Do the crimes warrant the severity implied? There are, perhaps, other ways to encourage "righteous" behavior besides threats of eternal punishment.

In chapter 9, I will address the general tone of John 3, but I want to turn your attention to it in this context as well. I hope you will read that chapter, thinking about how Jesus comes across in it. If you saw an actor portraying this chapter, what emotions might he employ to carry it off? Additionally, look for any ways that Jesus' words are violent or threatening. How would you characterize the Jesus depicted in this chapter?

Many people assume that everything that Jesus says in the Gospels is kind and loving, and this mind-set determines how they read and interpret the Gospels. I think it is essential to be able to try to set aside what you expect to find in order to be able to see what is really happening in there.

Words of Paul

Let's look at a few passages from Paul's letters. Keep in mind that Paul and his associates only wrote a letter to a church group that he had established (with the exception of the letter to the Romans), and only in response to questions that arose in his absence. So each of Paul's letters were quite specific and written without being able to assess the situations in person.

I will never forget the day that I heard a kind, soft-spoken undergraduate say to me how much she loved the passage in Romans where Paul tells people to be kind to their enemies, and in this way they will "heap burning coals" on their heads (Rom. 12:20). Even taken metaphorically, as it is surely intended, does it seem kind to wish that your enemies will be so frustrated by your kindness that it will feel like their heads are on fire? Think about how it is possible for a gentle, loving person to affirm such a passage in the Bible, without any sense of irony or hypocrisy. Interestingly enough, this verse is surrounded by admonishments neither to be overcome by evil nor to repay "evil for evil." I can't help but wonder if Paul saw heaping burning coals on heads as a loving gesture or as an exception to his advice to be honorable. You might find Romans 12 worth a close read.

Who Is My Enemy?

It seems to me that the notion of thinking of anyone as an "enemy" is worth reconsidering.

It is unsettling to me every time I see this word in the Bible, given how the words and worldview of the Bible shape the mindset of the people who read it. Even though there are passages that encourage people to "love your enemies," some people are still being called *enemies*. This word implies something inherently negative about them, which justifies animosity or hatred toward them. Labelling people as *enemies* keeps us from seeing the good in them or from believing that they are capable of anything good. It prevents us from acknowledging the humanity that we share.

As long as we speak about people as "friend or foe," "ally or enemy," we ensure that taking sides and fighting will continue. Where is the peace in that?

Pay attention, though, to the way some people are referred to as "enemies." Not just in Paul's letters, which is often enough, or Jesus' words (Matt. 5:43–48; Luke 5:27–36), but throughout the Bible. Notice how this way of seeing people is often a part of the underlying worldview of these passages. Labels and categories are powerful and affect the way we interact with people.

Here are a handful of other Pauline passages that you might want to read open-mindedly. Galatians 2:1–14 describes a circumcision issue among the Gentile followers of Jesus and an interaction between Paul and Peter (also called Cephas) because of it. Picture the scene and decide whether Paul is being gentle and kind in the way he corrects Peter, or . . . something else.

Try reading 1 Corinthians 5:1–8. The scenario Paul is denouncing is that a man is sleeping with his "father's wife," most likely the man's step-mom. Regardless of the behavior being discussed, pay attention to what Paul says, the shaming language, the lack of forgiveness extended to this "sexually immoral" person, even the way Paul asserts his own authority (esp. in vv. 3–5).

Looking back on these few passages from the Newer Testament, I would invite you to think about what it means that there are passages that perhaps were written with some pretty intense frustration behind them. There are passages that convey an angry tone or hatred toward other people. There are passages that show Paul being manipulative. All these are right there in the Bible serving as examples for people to emulate. Do you think that is right or helpful?

CONCLUSION

Whether it is "just for entertainment" in action movies or as elements in video games, I am not a fan of violence. So you might say that I am too sensitive to this topic to be writing with any objectivity about it. But I happen to think it is just the opposite. I am afraid that many people overlook the violence in the Bible because violence is so commonplace today. If we can be numb to the actual harm of any of the violence around us, today, then we will similarly miss the possible implications of it as portrayed in scripture.

Many people are unaware of the numerous forms of violence and manipulation that are depicted in scripture or that are described as the way God interacts with humankind. Many of these people seek guidance from the Bible, in various ways. If the texts people read endorse violent or manipulative ways of interacting, won't the people who read them end up doing the same? Perhaps not gang-raping a woman, but shaming and rejecting those one perceives as "sinners"? These are things that I hope you will give some thought. Permission granted.

 TAKE THE BIBLE INTO YOUR OWN HANDS

1. What impact does the battle imagery and language in the Bible have on our world today? Where do you see "God is on our side"

thinking playing out today? How might the world be different if we did not picture God as taking sides?

2. Do you believe God kills people, as punishment or for any other reason? What do you do with scriptures that describe God killing people or commanding people to kill other people?

3. What do the premises behind the sacrificial system say about God and humans? Do you think Jesus believed a bloody death (of animals or himself) was necessary for atonement?

4. Can you think of ways to encourage righteous living or loving behaviors that do not draw on threats of death or eternal punishments?

5. What do the stories of violence against women in scripture tell you about the world in which the Bible was written? What role does God play in those stories, if any?

6

Cover-Ups and Edited Stories

Most of the stories discussed in this chapter are familiar ones—familiar because they have been told to us our entire lives, from early childhood onward. Taking the Bible into your own hands, you may discover that the version of the story that you know is somewhat edited or sugar-coated compared to what is actually in the Bible. It can be frustrating, wondering why we were told a certain version as children but never given the adult version as we grew up. We want to believe that our Sunday school teachers and pastors meant well. But sitting there as adults long past our teens, only now finding out the full scoop, it can feel as if we have been lied to.

The stories we will discuss here involve the Exodus from Egypt, several stories related to David, Samson, Jonah, Job, Mary Magdalene, and that well-loved passage: John 3:16. While my intention here is to point out some of the juicy details you have been missing all these years, I do hope you will think about what all this means in terms of how you view the Bible.

EXODUS: FREEDOM, AT WHAT COST?

The story of Exodus, of God delivering the Israelites from slavery in Egypt, is central to the overall narrative of the Bible. Because it says that God chooses to side with the oppressed and hears the cries of his people, it is perhaps the most poignant and enduring message of God's love for his people in the Bible. This message has resonated with people in many life situations throughout the centuries, including today.

I direct your attention to it, then, because of the components that we tend to overlook. The Israelites are able to escape from Egypt because God intervenes in two significant ways. The first is by distracting the Egyptians with the deaths of the firstborn of their children and livestock. The second is by stopping the Egyptians' pursuit of the fleeing Israelites, causing thousands of soldiers and horses to die in the Red Sea. When you think about these two events from the perspective of the Egyptians, the tradition of Passover (based on Exodus 11–13) seems a lot less like something to celebrate. I must note that I have dear family and friends who are Jewish, and I have celebrated the Seder (Passover meal) with some of them. Writing about this passage gives me quite a heavy heart.

The final plague did not affect the Israelites because God gave them a signal. The angel of death knew to *pass over* those who had smeared the blood of a lamb on their doorposts. Today, when Passover is celebrated, the celebration focuses on deliverance, not on the death of all those Egyptian children, soldiers, and livestock. But the name comes from the final plague. God spared the lives of Israelites when taking the lives of many others.

I do wonder to what extent this kind of a story influences the way people today think about resolving conflicts and struggles for power. Where are the stories giving us examples of working out differences without people dying over it? Children take from this story whatever they are told to notice. But I assure you that, sooner or later, they will want to talk about the Egyptians' plight as well.

KING DAVID

David as king over Israel and fighter of giants holds a place of honor or much fondness in many people's hearts and faith. There is, of course, good reason for it. He was the first well-loved king over the united tribes of Israel, and God gave David the promise that one of his descendants would always be on the throne in Israel. David was the youngest of eight brothers and, as the story goes, was quite a scrappy and resourceful little guy. He is known for his musical abilities, songwriting gift, and ability to humble himself before God. That is not a bad résumé.

So why am I picking on David, of all people? There is much more to his story than most people realize. It also makes me nervous when anyone is put on a pedestal. Was David a "man after God's heart"? Perhaps he was. There is a moment when he realizes an action of his has caused harm to others, and he heartily repents. But that one moment does not define him entirely. I am interested in putting David in perspective. Are you game?

David and Goliath

This is perhaps one of the most beloved stories that we teach to children from the Hebrew Bible. The idea of a pint-sized boy slaying a giant resonates with just about anyone who has been an underdog. The name *Goliath* has become synonymous with any seemingly unsurmountable hurdle in a person's life, or with the powerhouse team that is unbeatable, and so forth. The idea behind this story is meaningful for people.

The story most people are familiar with is found in 1 Samuel 16–17. It begins with the narration of David being anointed as the king to succeed Saul. Part of the message is that the LORD looks not to the

---

Evil Spirits from the LORD?

In 1 Samuel 16, we get some fascinating insights into how people in David's time believed that God interacted with people as well as a view on "good and evil" that might surprise you.

1 Samuel 16:14 says, "Now the spirit of the LORD departed from Saul, and an evil spirit from the LORD tormented him." Hmmm. Why does the LORD choose to depart from Saul, much less torment Saul with an evil spirit? Do you think that God controls both good and evil spirits, as the author seems to think?

I bring this to your attention to highlight that the way "good and evil" is discussed in the Bible changes over time. In Samuel, God is responsible for both good and evil. In other parts of the Bible, the devil is responsible for evil. In still others, evil is not attributed to any spiritual being but to humans entirely.

This is one example of many in the Bible where we can see a belief changing over time. There is documented progression and development of thought within the Bible.

externals, as people tend to do, but to what a person is made of in their character. This anointing scene is followed by the battle scene where David ends up killing Goliath (1 Sam. 17).

As you read through 1 Samuel 17, pay attention to David's tendency to exaggerate. He claims that he literally took down lions and bears and tore them to pieces (17:34–37). I love that the human imagination can allow us to believe that David actually did those things. But as encounters with lions and bears indicate, this was pure storytelling meant to celebrate David as a hero, not a literal description of superhuman strength. I think you do David's story more justice when you read it in light of the way it was intended to affect the reader/hearer instead of believing it all to be literally true.

These and other exaggerated stories are trying to get people on board with the idea of David as the next king. They are a part of an ancient campaign program: "This guy was chosen by God. His music calms those with disturbed spirits! He can bare-handedly kill lions and tigers and bears, oh my! He is not frightened when facing Israel's enemies. . . . He is your next King!" You can let these stories function as political propaganda without insisting that they actually happened.

Consider 1 Samuel 17 in comparison to 2 Samuel 21 and 1 Chronicles 20. (Chronicles summarizes the main events that we find in Genesis through Samuel.) In chart 2, I have given only the summary of the elements related to Goliath, the size of his spear, and who is noted to have done the killing of Goliath. Please read the full passages for clarity, keeping in mind that saying that Goliath is from Gath is another way of saying "Goliath the Gittite."

By comparing these three stories, I hope that you noticed these four things. 1) All versions refer to a Goliath from Gath. 2) There is a spear involved, whose shaft was the size of a weaver's beam. 3) Three different men are attributed with killing Goliath, assuming he is even killed in all three versions. 4) There are enough parallels among these stories that they appear to be drawing on the same original event. The differences in details do not have to be devastating to the value we place on scripture, however, since we know that biblical stories are, in large part, myth. What is happening is a natural result of passing along stories for hundreds of years, as these were, before writing them down.

I remember the day someone suggested to me the possibility that David was not actually the person who killed Goliath. It felt something like the last straw. I was so tired of learning that things in the Bible were not as I had always thought of them. Like the person who dropped that

Chart 2: Who Killed Goliath?

1 Samuel 17: 4–11

In this version of the story, Goliath of Gath, whose height was six cubits and a span, is the only giant mentioned. His armor is described. The spear like a weaver's beam is his and the head of the spear is six hundred shekels of iron. Goliath is clearly the one taunting Israel. David is the one to kill him.

2 Samuel 21:15–22

In this version of the story, it is Ishbibenob's spear whose weight is given, and it is three hundred shekels of bronze. He is also the giant to threaten David's life. Abishai, not David, kills him. It is Elhanan who kills Goliath the Gittite, whose spear was like a weaver's beam. Jonathan killed the giant who is said to have taunted Israel. This giant is unnamed but is noted to have had six fingers on each hand and six toes on each foot. There are four giants, total, named and killed in this version, but David kills none of them.

1 Chronicles 20:4–8

Here, Elhanan kills Lahmi, the brother of Goliath. One of them— Lahmi or Goliath, it is not clear which—had a spear like a weaver's beam. Another giant is noted to be six-toed and six-fingered, and he is the one who taunted Israel. Jonathan is said to have killed this giant. It is not clear that Goliath is even killed, though it may be implied that Jonathan kills him.

"last straw" on me did, let me remind you that I am not trying to poke holes in anyone's faith. On the contrary, it can enrich one's faith to read passages in the Bible in a way that respects the purposes for which they were written. In this case, the idea of defeating giants worked well to bolster David's reputation. It is best to keep in mind what it was that the stories were trying to accomplish rather than insisting that they actually took place as narrated.

David and Bathsheba

Moving ahead in David's life a few chapters, we find the story involving Bathsheba. If you are familiar with this story, I invite you to think about the associations you have with her name. Is she a temptress trying to catch David's eye? Is she an innocent victim? How does this encounter fit into David's overall story and reputation?

As you read 2 Samuel 11–12, read slowly enough to allow each scene to play out on your mental movie screen. The opening verse suggests that David has shirked his responsibilities as the leader of the army. The music in the background is perhaps a bit edgy and ominous, with that foreshadowing-of-doom kind of quality. Pay close attention to David's choices, and try to see it all from Bathsheba's perspective.

Did you notice what David did when he saw a beautiful woman performing her ritual cleansing? When informed that she was already someone else's wife, he still ordered that she be brought to him so he could have sex with her. I have heard people suggest that she was trying to seduce David. Did you see that? Furthermore, David being king meant that Bathsheba had no say in this situation. There are many possibilities for how their first encounter played out: perhaps she was flattered by the request and went willingly or perhaps she was taken by force and raped, but whatever the case, she could not refuse the wishes of the king. Regardless, I hope you understand why I would challenge anyone who wants to pin the responsibility on Bathsheba.

When Bathsheba hears of the death of her husband, she mourns for him. What do you think her response was when David sent for her again in order to marry her? Depending on how you read their first encounter, this could be the happiest day of her life, some form of relief for being looked after in her widowhood, or a frightening development.

I hope you will read chapter 12 as well. Most people are surprised to see that David has offended the LORD because he has taken another man's property: Bathsheba. Notice also how Bathsheba is punished, time and again, because of David's choices.

This whole story is, of course, quite telling of the view of women at the time, which should not surprise us. However, this behavior reflects on David as a role model overall. For me the icing on the cake is that Psalm 51 was written after this event, attributed to David. It is, in my opinion, the most powerful psalm in the Psalter. In it, David is contrite; he is deeply sorry for what he did. But in the psalm, he says he has sinned only against God, with no mention of wrong done to Bathsheba, her dead husband, or her dead child. Ouch.

We should also note that in the retelling of the story of Israel in Chronicles, Bathsheba is not even mentioned. It is not just that she is not named and just referred to as "Uriah's wife," as we see in the Newer Testament; the story itself is not retold. The story that led to calling

David "a man after God's heart," is not even included the second time around.

Finally, it is stunning to me how often women in biblical stories have reputations with strikingly negative sexual connotations that are unfounded by scripture. For instance, after reading this story and thinking about it for yourself, would you put Bathsheba among the *Really Bad Girls of the Bible,* as author Liz Curtis Higgs does?

David and Tamar

The final story from David's saga is much less well known than the first two. It involves three of his children: the siblings Absalom and Tamar, and Amnon, David's first son and half-brother to the other two. The story will be (slightly) less creepy if you keep this half-sibling relation in mind.

The opening line of 2 Samuel 13 tells us that Amnon was in love with his beautiful (half-)sister, Tamar. Oh dear. If you are wondering if David's oldest son has picked up any of his father's ways with women, you are tracking with the cues correctly.

As with other stories, try to picture each scene, starting with Amnon seeking relationship advice and what is recommended. Any parents reading this, please picture Tamar as your beautiful, perhaps mid-teens daughter whose presence is requested in the bedroom of an older man, in order to fix some food and feed it to him. Even though they are siblings, given the nature of the intimacy implied here, I have a hunch you might not respond to this situation as David does. Regardless, as you read about the interaction between Amnon and Tamar, try to imagine what the whole scene might have been like for her. (Go read 2 Sam. 13:1–19.) What crossed your mind in light of Amnon's lustful stare or beckoning her into his bedroom? Did you notice all the things she says in trying to deter him from raping her? One piece you might not have anticipated, which leaves me frozen every time, is: "Now therefore, I beg you, speak to the king; for he will not withhold me from you" (2 Sam. 13:13).

Was she really willing to marry her half-brother, who was trying to rape her in that moment?! Perhaps it was just a stall tactic. Regardless, he raped her anyway. According to 2 Samuel 13:21, David was angry to hear of this development but did not punish Amnon. Neither does he go to comfort Tamar. David's own daughter is raped by his own son, and he does nothing in response.

This is the point I am most interested in raising about this story: regardless of whether we view women differently today than they did "back then," there are still moments such as this one in scripture. David's example here brings me close to tears, every time. I know that there are people today who overlook the harm done to someone they love when it is done by the hand of another loved one. I understand that it is scary and confusing to address such a delicate situation. But please, for the love of all that is good, we must not let scripture's silence in response to a rape (or other form of abuse) be a model for us today.

Conclusion on David Stories

It literally brings me to tears every time I spend time in one of these rape or abuse stories in the Bible. These stories, among others, immediately come to mind whenever I hear someone say, "I believe in the Bible." Usually a person who says this tends to believe that everything in it is as God intended, therefore it is all good. For many people, this is the ultimate way of respecting the Bible. But it seems to me that they aren't actually respecting the Bible because they are not taking it seriously *enough*. Not everything in the Bible is good and worth emulating. As stories such as these about David indicate, not everything in the Bible was inspired by God. If horrible, terrible things such as David's procuring of Bathsheba and lack of response to the rape of his daughter were inspired by God, then please cease and desist from worshiping that God.

You also might want to think of David as a complicated human instead of being purely a "man after God's heart."

SAMSON

The full story of Samson can be found in Judges 13–17. Samson is one of the judges chosen by God to lead Israel for a time. As with other somewhat familiar stories, please take a moment to take stock of this story for yourself. What parts of it do you remember? Is there a "moral to the story," or is it just an entertaining story to tell children?

As you read this story, remember that God forbade the Israelites from marrying non-Israelite women. This decree makes Judges 14:4 somewhat remarkable. Apparently, the LORD caused Samson to fall in love with a foreign woman, a Philistine, in order to justify harming the Philistines as a people. Hmmm. Fascinating motivations and actions attributed to God here.

Judges 14–15 are usually unfamiliar to people, so pay attention to the way Samson's actions are being described and where his strength comes from. Do you find his reactions justifiable? Most disturbing, Samson's intense anger is merely the instrument of God's wrath against the Philistines, since it is described as the Spirit of the LORD rushing on him. There are so many details in these two chapters worth chewing on, for the sake of putting Samson in perspective.

The rest of Samson's story, in Judges 16–17, is the more familiar part. As you read these chapters, consider how such exchanges between Samson and Delilah could be possible. "Fool me once, shame on you; fool me three times. . . ." (?!) Additionally, note what is said about Samson, since the women in his life constantly "nag" him. This observation might evoke a giggle or chortle from you, but in all seriousness, it belittles everyone to perpetuate this kind of portrayal of men and women. I would like to think that adults can communicate much better than Samson seems to with his wives.

I have heard people speak in awe of Samson's courage for the way he dies. The thing is, his final act is both a suicide and an act of vengeance. As I type that last line, reports of recent suicide bombers run through my mind. The more I read this story, the more difficult it is for me to find something useful in it: Samson has rage and retaliation issues, is freak-of-nature strong without being able to keep it in check, and seems to be unable to have healthy relationships with women. Which part of Samson's story do we want children emulating?

Originally, Samson's story was part of indicating that having a judge such as him ruling over Israel was not sufficient, which helped to justify having a king. But that is not normally the "takeaway" from Samson's story. Instead, people think of it as a story warning not to waste the gifts God gave you, or, more frequently, as a warning about staying away from sultry women and keeping your lusts in check. Things for you to ponder. Permission granted.

JONAH AND THE "WHALE"

The story of Jonah is another one that many people have a general sense of, either from growing up coloring pictures of large fish to stay busy during worship services or just from hearing about it in passing. When I ask people what their sense of the message of Jonah's story is, the answer is always some version of, "Obey God, and everything will be okay." Take a moment to check in on your understanding of the story of Jonah before reading any further.

The book of Jonah is only four chapters, so it is easy to read in one sitting. (Hint, hint.) The parts most people are familiar with—Jonah running from a task and being swallowed then regurgitated by a large fish—are contained in the first two chapters. But, as stories go, we need to keep reading in order to get the whole point. In the remainder of the story, Jonah comes across as a bit petty or even pouty and childish. See what you think.

If you read closely, you will notice that the main issue is not about Jonah needing to learn to obey. It is about God choosing to be loving and kind to another group of people beyond the Israelites. And not just any group of people, but the Ninevites, who were sworn enemies of the Israelites at the time. This message does not show up in the Bible very often—a fact that, in itself, might surprise you, given how much emphasis we put on Jesus' teaching to this effect. The thing is, this message is in the story from beginning to end (see esp. 1:1–3; 3:1–5, 10; 4:1–5). Why do you suppose we have crafted the message of Jonah to overlook this message that even our "enemies" are humans too, and deserving of God's care?

JOB

Job is another one of the iconic characters from the Bible. Most people have heard about him and usually have some sense of his patience or faith being tested. Take a moment to think of any of the ideas you associate with Job. What is the message of Job's story?

In the first five verses of Job, the narrator paints a picture of Job and his character. Give yourself a moment to get a good sense of Job. If he was your neighbor, how might you perceive him, for instance?

The heading in my Bible for the next section is "Attack on Job's Character." This is a great example of why it is important to be aware that the headings, which were made up (except in Psalms) and added to our Bibles, affect the way we read a story. Those headings are intended to help you make sense of the story. After reading these verses for yourself, you might choose a different heading.

As you read the next section, Job 1:6–12, it is helpful to understand the "Satan" character appropriately (see the discussion of "Satan" on pp. 28–29). I like to call this character "*ha-satan*," since that is what it is in the Hebrew. It is a role, not a name. A "satan" is an advocate or counselor, as in the types we would find in a court of law. It is from this story that we get the idea of "the devil's advocate." But playing the devil's advocate simply means bringing some perspective to a situation.

In Job 1:6, we see that God's advisors gather. Think of this in terms of the president's daily Cabinet meetings, sharing information and debriefing recent developments. In Job's story, these advisors are technically labeled "sons of God" in the Hebrew. This is not to say that David or Jesus was there; rather that this label, "son of God," is used in lots of ways in the Bible.

Please read Job 1:6–12 slowly and thoughtfully. Set aside any notion of *ha-satan* being evil or out to get Job, or anyone else for that matter. What does it tell you that God turns to *ha-satan* first in this morning advisory meeting? Pay attention to the way God talks about Job. Hopefully you can see that *ha-satan* says what any good friend would say, which is the hard thing to say. *Ha-satan*, playing the original "devil's advocate," is merely pointing out what might be naïveté on God's part.

Also worth noting, if you finish reading chapter 1, is that it is God, not *ha-satan*, who is responsible for what happens to Job and his family members.

The book of Job is not primarily about teaching us to be faithful in the midst of trials. But neither is Job's story about God testing our faith or sending trials to strengthen it. It is actually trying to address something much more complex than these two ideas.

This story was written to challenge a belief that had held sway in the Israelites' scriptures up until that point (concentrated in Deut.–2 Kgs.). The people of Israel had been taught that if they kept their end of the covenant with God, then God would take care of and protect them. If they neglected their part of the covenant, God would cause or allow bad things to happen to them.

The book of Job depicts Job as a model of keeping the covenant with God, yet terrible things happen to him anyway. Job's story was written to put this life experience, which contradicts what they had previously believed, in a story form. The fact that Job never curses God simply drives home the point that sometimes bad things happen to "good" people, for absolutely no reason.

So please take note. Some of the writings in the Bible say that if something bad happens to you, it is your fault, and God has allowed it to happen to you (Jdg. 2:11–23; 3:7–11; 4:1–3; 1 Sam. 12:19–25; Isa. 65:11–12; 66:1–4). The book of Job challenges this belief altogether.

MARY MAGDALENE

Before we look at the few references to Mary Magdalene in the Newer Testament, do take a moment to take stock of your own impression of who Mary was or the things you associate with her. What was her relationship to Jesus, or why was she important? Do you know where you got those ideas?

The story of Mary Magdalene fits in this chapter for slightly different reasons than the previous stories do. Hers is an example of getting two stories in scripture confused or combined, and this combination made it into the collective memory of the Church. What I tend to hear, when I ask what people associate with her, is that she had seven demons driven out of her (true), she was close to Jesus (true), she anointed Jesus' feet (not true—different Mary), and most often, that she was a prostitute (not true).

One might wonder, then, how we all got this perception that she was a prostitute and that so many shelters and programs for former prostitutes/sex workers are called "Magdalene House" or something similar. Why? Because somewhere in Church history, some men blended Mary's story with the unnamed woman (perhaps prostitute) in Luke 7:36–50, added to it the version of the anointing of Jesus' feet by a *different* Mary, and passed along the blend as if it was "gospel truth." Perhaps the question you should be asking is, "Why would they do that to Mary and her reputation?"

Of course, we will never be able to answer this question. What we do know is that there was an early tradition that said that Mary Magdalene and Jesus had a close bond, even closer than his with his disciples. It also said that she had insights from Jesus that the other disciples did not. In fact, she is depicted as more prominent among the disciples than Peter, who becomes the "rock" on which the Church is built. Given the direction the Church took on women's roles by the end of the first century, it would make sense to want to hide the importance of a woman so close to Jesus. But Mary's reputation was maligned within the writings of the early Church Fathers, not within the Bible itself.

Think of all the people who have believed, wholeheartedly, that Mary Magdalene was a prostitute. Millions of people have taken an idea from the early Church Fathers and treated it as scripture. This misrepresentation of Mary is one of many "biblical beliefs" that are not grounded in scripture.

There are not many references to Mary Magdalene in the Newer Testament. Matthew, Mark, and John do not mention her until the very end, at the crucifixion and the empty tomb. We could say that she is central to the tomb scene, however. The list of women who go to the tomb that morning varies between the four Gospels, but all include Mary. According to John's Gospel, she is the only one who goes to discover the empty tomb!

Luke's Gospel gives us an important tidbit about Mary Magdalene. Luke 8:1–3 tells us that Mary and some other women also traveled with Jesus, along with the twelve male disciples. It is in this passage that we are told that she had seven evil spirits driven out of her, and that is all that is said about her. There is no mention of her profession (current or former).

What many people want to discuss is what those seven evil spirits represent or what the significance of seven was. We cannot know for sure what was originally intended. Some scholars suggest that the number seven is the significant part, since it indicates perfection. Thus she was either entirely demon possessed or she was entirely healed. Movie producers, scholars, and pastors alike have tried to assign the "seven deadly sins" or "seven venal sins" to those seven spirits, as seen in Cecil B. DeMille's 1927 production, *King of Kings*. Regardless of how you make sense of those spirits, they were driven out of her. As anyone who cannot shake a childhood nickname will tell you, it is counterproductive to keep focusing on her potentially negative past instead of on who she had become.

But did you notice what was said in Luke 8:3? Apparently Mary, Joanna, Susanna, and many other women financed the travels of Jesus and the twelve male disciples. Jesus had a band of sugar mamas! This inclusion in Luke also tells us that when you see a reference to "Jesus and his disciples" in the Gospels, it is appropriate to imagine at least a handful of women disciples in the scene as well. If you give that some thought, it might radically change the way you envision Jesus and some of the stories in the Gospels.

It seems that the Church Fathers got the idea that Mary was a prostitute by combining the Luke 8:1–3 reference to Mary with the story immediately prior to it, in Luke 7:36–50. That story is one of the three anointing scenes (in all the Gospels except for Mark) where a woman pours oil on Jesus in a semi-public setting. What most people are not aware of, however, are the variations among the three versions of it. Chart 3 should help you see what I mean.

Chart 3: Who Anointed Jesus' Feet?

Matthew 26:6–13
This scene depicts an unnamed woman living in Bethany who visits Jesus while he is at Simon the leper's house. She pours costly ointment on Jesus' head. Jesus says her action is done in preparation for his burial.

Luke 7:36–50
This unnamed woman is described as "a woman in the city, a sinner." She visits Jesus while he is at a Pharisee's house. She pours the oil on his feet. The action is part of a larger message of forgiveness, an important theme in Luke.

John 12:1–3
The woman is Mary, of the "Martha and Mary" pair. Jesus is in Lazarus's house in Bethany. Mary anoints his feet with the pure nard. Jesus indicates that she is doing that in preparation for his burial.

You can see why these stories get a bit jumbled!

Some have suggested that it is odd to think of this scene actually transpiring three different times, and I would agree. The discrepancy in details is best explained as a natural part of storytelling, adapting some parts of an event for the immediate audience. Respecting scripture, in this case, means moving beyond believing that all three versions happened to seeing the meaning of the story in each context.

As you read Luke 7:36–50, pay attention to the woman. She is not named but is described as "a woman in the city, who was a sinner." Since there are plenty of ways of "sinning," many people question why this label means that she was specifically a sex worker. Perhaps "sinner" was a euphemism for prostitute when applied to women (for some people, it still is!). "You know, she is one of those . . . sinners," and at the time people would have known exactly what that meant. There is also the issue of how women were viewed at the time. Since they were primarily talked about according to their status as a wife, daughter, or virgin, with the concern being about their sexual usefulness, it is not difficult to see how a woman "sinning," according to men, would be a transgression of how her sexuality was employed.

I will admit that this explanation makes the most sense to me, not only for these reasons, but also because of the way the woman interacts with Jesus in this story. Picture it carefully. It was typical for the men around a table to recline or be mostly horizontal, which was how she could stand "behind him" and get to his feet so easily. Imagine her cleaning his feet with her tears, wiping them with her hair, kissing them. This is incredibly intimate and sensual. Sex workers, then as now, would have oil on hand to use in their profession, and she had oil to bring with her for this interaction.

One thing is clear: the woman in this scene is not named and we have no reason to assume that she is Mary Magdalene. In fact, since Mary is named in the very next chapter, it seems odd not to make the connection clear, had there been one.

Take a moment to think about what happened when the early Church Fathers combined these two stories, making it seem like Mary was the woman cleaning and anointing Jesus' feet. There are (at least) two pieces to consider here. The first is that some of the interpretations of the Bible, by men in the early Church, have lived on quite powerfully. The second is that this happened in spite of those interpretations not being backed up by scripture. Things to think about. Permission granted.

FOR GOD SO LOVED THE WORLD . . .

Perhaps the best known biblical passage, by chapter and verse, is John 3:16. I make this entirely unsupported-by-research guess based on how often sports cams scan over fans with it painted on their faces or bodies, not to mention on the athletes' cheeks. Then there are the bumper stickers, tattoos, billboards, and church signs that all announce this verse. Regardless of the medium, I am never certain if it is intended as a reminder, an invitation, or a warning. The mixture of the seriousness of the message and the often silly ways it is presented do make me pause. How exactly are people supposed to hear and respond to this verse?

Please take a moment to think through your own thoughts on this passage. What is the basic message? Perhaps it gives you warm fuzzies,

Mary, Mary, and Many Others

The presence of many Marys in the Gospels has been a cause of confusion for many people, so a short discussion seems appropriate. The list goes something like this:

Mary, mother of Jesus. In the birth announcement scenes (Matt. 1–2, Luke 1–2) she is simply called "Mary." Most of the time in the Gospels she is referred to as his mother. It gets a bit dicey sorting through who is mentioned at the crucifixion and empty-tomb scenes, but it seems that she is at the crucifixion and in three of the four empty-tomb scenes.

Mary Magdalene. The name "Magdalene" tells us that she is from Magdala. She shows up in Luke 8:1–3 and then at the crucifixion and tomb scenes in all four Gospels. In John, she is the first person to interact with Jesus post-resurrection, which is actually a rather big deal. She is also always listed first, even before Jesus' mother, in any of the lists of women mentioned.

Mary, sister to Martha. Luke 10:38–42 has the story where Martha fixes food while her sister Mary sits at Jesus' feet learning from him. That makes Mary a disciple of Jesus. (Contrary to popular belief, this is not something unique to Jesus. There were other rabbis at the time who taught women.) It appears that they are the same "Martha and Mary" who are siblings of Lazarus, mentioned in John 11. It is this Mary who anoints Jesus' feet in John 12 prior to his arrest and crucifixion.

Mary, the mother of James. This is a tricky one. Three times in Mark there is a reference to a Mary in this way. (Mark 6:3, 15:10 and 16:1; also in Luke 24:10). It seems that these are most likely references to the same person. According to Mark 6:3, it is Jesus' own mother. Why is she not just called "Mary, mother of Jesus"? Good question!

"The other Mary." This is how the previous Mary is referred to in a couple places, once she has been introduced as "Mary, mother of James." Note that this is most likely Jesus' mother, and the primary Mary being talked about is Mary Magdalene. Like it or not, Mary Magdalene has place of privilege over Jesus' mother.

Mary, Jesus' mother's sister, and wife of Clopas. (John 19:25)

Mary, the mother of John, whose other name was Mark. (Acts 12: 12)

You can see why this discussion of Marys gets a bit confusing at times!

thinking of how much God loves everyone. But what if you are among the people who do not believe in the Son?

Here is the verse, in full:

> For God so loved the world that he gave his only Son, so that everyone who believes in him might not perish but have eternal life.

One of the things I warned against in the first chapter is taking verses out of context. This is one of those passages. See for yourself. Does your understanding of John 3:16 change if you read 3:17–18 along with it?

> Indeed, God did not send the Son into the world to condemn the world, but in order that the world might be saved through him. Those who believe in him are not condemned; but those who do not believe are condemned already, because they have not believed in the name of the only Son of God.

Many people point out that the content of 3:17–18 should not surprise us, since it is somewhat implied in 3:16. Absolutely. Though saying that people are already condemned does raise questions regarding trying to make converts at all, doesn't it?

What I would encourage you to do is to read through all of John 3, thinking about the way God is depicted, which influences how people relate to this God. Notice the final verse of John 3: "Whoever believes in the Son has eternal life; whoever disobeys the Son will not see life, but must endure God's wrath." There is quite a bit of God's wrath discussed or implied in this section of John.

What does it say that God is fine with subjecting some of the people he has created to his own divine wrath? This believe-or-suffer tactic is not only pretty intense; it is also entirely off-putting to many people, with good reason! This is not love being offered freely. It is "love me or else." That qualifies as a threat. Today, we tend to encourage people to stay out of relationships based on this kind of a dynamic; we label them as manipulative or abusive.

John 3:16, the passage that people take to refer to God's love, is actually part of a larger depiction of a God who uses fear tactics and threats to get people to love and follow him. This is additionally interesting, given that at least one letter in the Newer Testament talks about love driving out fear and that there is no fear in love (1 John 4:18). Hmmm.

Let me be clear: I do not think that God is actually full of threats and wrath. But that is how God is being depicted. This is another one of those moments where it is helpful to be able to say that some of scripture reflects human ideas more than those of God. The thought of people worshiping a God who literally scares people into loving him concerns me. It is also unsettling that people find a way to defend this depiction of God just because it is in scripture.

CONCLUSION

These discussions have, in the past, pushed some people to think about what it says about the Bible that some of the stories must be so heavily edited in order to teach them to children. They have raised questions regarding what one can expect to find in the Bible. Perhaps most unsettling for some people, these discussions highlight that sometimes what they thought was a biblical idea is simply not in there at all.

Seeing any part of the Bible differently than you did before does not change who God is or what is in the Bible. It might change the way the Bible helps you relate to that God. It might, also, change your view of who God is. I hope for the better.

Permission granted.

 TAKE THE BIBLE INTO YOUR OWN HANDS

1. What do you think is the impact of teaching children less-graphic versions or feel-good morals of stories that we see as adults are much more complex? How should we handle stories (such as the Passover) that seem to gloss over terrible violence and suffering?

2. How do you make sense of multiple versions of the same or similar stories? The killing of Goliath, the women anointing Jesus, and Genesis 1–2 (discussed in chap. 2) may fall into this category.

3. How or why do you think so many people have missed the intended point of stories such as those about Samson, Jonah, and Job?

4. What are some side effects of making someone seem overwhelmingly virtuous (such as David) or of taking just the positive elements from complex passages (such as John 3:16–18)? How might our reading of the Bible be different if we took a more complex view of characters and claims about God?

7

Biblical Women: Silent, Submissive Baby Makers?

Women in the Bible: quite a hot topic. For various reasons, however, people tend to have fairly worked-through thoughts about the subject that can make approaching this conversation a bit tricky. I think it often feels as if there is a great deal at stake in having this particular conversation, and I suppose that that is actually the case! But as with any endeavor with a lot at stake, taking the time to carefully work through it can be quite rewarding. Are you game?

First, I encourage you to take a few moments to sort through what you have always heard or assumed that the Bible says that women should be or do. Which parts of a woman's life are addressed by the Bible, as far as you know? Are they the same kinds of things as are said directly to men? You might want to think about why the Bible makes distinctions in the content addressed to women or men.

In this chapter, one of the main ideas that should become clear is that instead of thinking of these stories as prescriptive, perhaps it is worth considering that many of these stories are simply descriptive. Prescriptive ideas are enduring ideals for women that should be maintained for all time; descriptive stories are merely describing how things were at that time.

Working somewhat chronologically, then, we'll begin by looking at the matriarchs of the Hebrew Bible, some other women in significant stories in the Hebrew Bible, women who were close to Jesus, and finally what the letters of Paul have to say about women. You might be in for a surprise!

MATRIARCHS OF THE BIBLE

The women I refer to as "the matriarchs" are the wives of the patriarchs. These are the men associated with the beginnings of the people
we call the Israelites, specifically Abraham, Isaac, and Jacob (whose
name changes to "Israel" in Gen. 32). Their wives are Sarah, Rebekah,
Rachel, and Leah. Yes, one of those men had two legitimate wives,
simultaneously. Hmmm. (For more thoughts about "biblical marriage," please see chap. 4.)

If we want to see what those first women were like and what it is
about being the wives of the patriarchs that is important, then we must
look to the stories in Genesis 12–50.

Sarah is the wife of Abraham (they are Sarai and Abram in early
stories). She is specifically mentioned in Genesis 11, 12, 16–18, 20,
and 21, always in light of creating children for Abraham or going along
with Abraham's plans. All other references to her in the Hebrew Bible
are in light of her being Abraham's wife, thus the implied mother of
all of Israel. Sarah gets a few Newer Testament references, found in
Romans 4:19; 9:9; Galatians 4:21; Hebrews 11:11; and 1 Peter 3:6.

I would like to draw your attention to Genesis 12. This story serves
as a great example of the treatment of the matriarchs in the Hebrew
Bible and is also indirectly referenced in 1 Peter 3, where Sarah's obedience and endurance of something terrifying is used as an example for
wives. So, as you read Genesis 12, look for the event that might be terrifying for Sarah and pay attention to Sarah's voice in this story.

How would you describe Abraham and Sarah's encounter with the
Pharaoh and his court? If you were thinking that the frightening part of
this story was about trying to stay alive, keep in mind that new induct-
ees to a concubinage would be required to "demonstrate their skills"
right away. In other words, Abraham essentially pimped out his wife
to spare himself and makes out like a bandit because of it. I'm not sure
which is more frightening: being forced to have sex with someone or
the way Abraham treats his wife/property. What do you think?

From the perspective of many rabbis, pastors, and biblical scholars, this
story tells us two things: 1) how Abraham came to have plenty of servants
and animals by which to survive in a new land and 2) the beginnings of
hard feelings between Abraham's descendants and the people of Egypt.

Unlike Abraham, who is held up throughout the Bible as a model of
faithfulness to God, Sarah is held up for her obedience to her husband
and her courage in frightening, physically abusive situations. Hmmm.

In terms of the other three matriarchs, I will suggest that you read their stories with similar curiosity. Rebekah's story begins in Genesis 24, and Rachel and Leah's begins in Genesis 29. Why are Rebekah, Rachel, and Leah chosen as wives for Isaac and Jacob? What I mean is, what does the narrator tell us about these women that makes them suitable wife material? Also pay attention to how often they get to participate or speak in their own stories. Do you see them talked about as important to the story in roles that go beyond being a mother?

Finally, there is a matter related to women beyond these four matriarchs that is worth your time to consider. Think about the message being sent about women and their importance in the world when we see them lamenting being childless. In saying this, I do not intend to belittle the genuine sadness that many women experience when learning that they are unable to conceive a child. But what do you sense the sorrow is all about for "barren" women in the Bible? Is it a longing for motherhood? Is it sadness or shame in not providing her husband with a son? Is it fear of not being able to survive in her later years without a son taking care of her? It is, in all honesty, most likely a combination of all these things. But I'd like to push you to think about how it all hinges on being a mother.

We see this in Sarah's story, as well as initially in Rebekah's and in Rachel's. But it happens several more times, almost as if God needing to intervene in women's wombs was an important part of the overarching biblical narrative. For instance: Samson's mother is "barren" until the LORD intervenes (Jdg. 13), and Hannah is shown to be in great despair over being childless (1 Sam. 1–2). It appears that Michal is cursed with barrenness for her sarcasm directed at David (2 Sam. 6). Isaiah 54:1–2, encouragement to barren women, would not be so meaningful if being barren weren't considered such a terrible thing. The story of John the Baptist begins by noting that his mother was assumed to be barren (Luke 1:7) prior to becoming pregnant with him. The need for levirate marriage was primarily about a man having children to carry on his name; taking care of the woman was secondary (as Tamar's story reminds us in Gen. 38). The fruitfulness of a woman's womb determined a great deal of her status and worth.

I would like to think that this particular way of viewing women had gone the way of dinosaurs, but alas, I can confirm that it continues today. I have lost track of the number of sad looks I have received, from well-meaning people, when they hear that I do not have children. Is there another way to interpret their sadness than that they perceive me to be unfortunate? Think about this. Please. These assumptions about women being unfulfilled without marriage and children are not just found in the Bible; they are alive and well today, due, in part, to such biblical messages.

OTHER HEBREW BIBLE WOMEN

Let's turn now to the stories of Deborah, Jael, Esther, and Ruth and Naomi, as well as the general valuation of women evidenced in the laws. If you are familiar with these women I have just named, take a moment to think about why they are hailed as important or as role models for women and girls today (or whether they are at all).

Deborah and Jael

These two women are found in Judges 4–5. Many people are familiar with Deborah, the one female noted as a judge over Israel. A judge held both decision-making and leadership responsibilities. This means that Deborah, as a judge and a prophetess for Israel, was a woman holding much power and respect.

I encourage you to read these two chapters of Judges, looking for clues about these two women's character or what they do that makes them exemplary. You might even want to think about the extent to which either of these women would fall into typical gender roles for women in your community.

For instance, when Barak refuses to go into battle without Deborah, why do you think this is? It might say something about Barak not being "fit to fight" or perhaps that Deborah was a shrewd and courageous fighter. Whatever the case, since Barak hesitates the LORD decides to deliver the enemy commander, Sisera, into the hands of a woman. Notice the layers of mockery or slights implied toward Barak in this development.

As you read about Jael, think about how intimate a space a person's tent is and consider all the sexual innuendo in her story. You should know that "tent" is one of the euphemisms for vaginas in the Hebrew Bible. Jael and Deborah save the day and are celebrated in song, just as other military leaders are celebrated in song throughout the Hebrew Bible. The violence and leadership of these women's actions place them outside gender norms at the time. As we saw for the matriarchs, however, we could also discuss why sex plays such an important role in this story.

Esther

Esther is one of the two women in the Hebrew Bible to have a book named after her. The other is Ruth, whom we will discuss next. The book of Esther contains the story explaining the origin of Purim, one of the festivals celebrated in the Jewish tradition. This book is short and

---

The "Pornification of Everything"

If you spent much time on Twitter in late 2013, you may have caught some of Rashida Jones's tweet fest about the "pornification of everything." Her concern, with which I agree, was about the degree to which female pop stars reveal certain "private parts" publicly and the amount and kind of suggestive gestures they are willing to perform in front of a camera. For years now, people have talked about how sex is used to sell practically everything. What Jones was commenting on was how this dynamic has reached new levels, almost to the point that such sexualization of oneself is required of female pop stars. She did, by the way, get a great deal of pushback on her comments, from both men and women.

I tell you all this because there are certain aspects of what Jones was critiquing, the focus on women's bodies and their usefulness sexually, that resonate with some of the messages we see in the Bible about women. In ancient times, women were rarely valued for their minds or talents and primarily valued for their sexual and reproductive abilities.

There is a sense of agency that is available to women today that simply did not exist in biblical times. Because of this, it is deeply saddening to me that so many women make choices that signal to others that they are worth seeing (in videos, on shows, on magazine covers, etc.) only if they tap into an overt form of sex appeal, or soft porn. These women buy into and perpetuate the idea that women are to be looked at, to be the objects of men's gaze.

So I urge you to think about the messages regarding women in the Bible. Given the power and influence that the Bible has for many people today, consciously or not, we do ourselves a favor to take seriously, and critique, the sexualization of women in the Bible.

pleasantly suspenseful, and only by reading it yourself will you be able to appreciate the depiction of Esther in this story.

As you read it, please be on the lookout for the following things. It seems that the reason Esther is chosen as the replacement queen has to do with the beautifying regimen she undergoes and because she is quite pleasing in the bedroom. Do you see other reasons? Many people have commented on how Esther seems to be a puppet, merely carrying out the plans of her uncle Mordecai, though it must be noted how much courage she had to have to see them through. What do you think?

Esther is a hero, no question. The celebration of Purim is complicated, though. Just as we see the death of thousands of Egyptians in the backdrop of the Passover, Purim celebrates the deliverance of the people of Israel at the cost of thousands of Persian lives. When you look at how Esther managed to influence events, however, you might want to ask why sex and seduction is again such an important part of the story. Which aspect of Esther's character or story do you celebrate today?

Ruth and Naomi

The book of Ruth tells the story of Ruth and Naomi. If you have heard of Ruth, please take a moment to decide for yourself what the "message" of this story is and thus why Ruth is so important.

What I find most interesting about Ruth's story are the following two things. First, her plea to Naomi that she be allowed to follow Naomi back to her homeland included poetic lines so intimate, personal, and beautiful that they are often read in wedding ceremonies today. Think about this for a moment. This was a deep love. Even Ruth's devotion to the God of the Israelites is proclaimed in light of her love for Naomi, not the other way around.

The second thing about Ruth's story that I find interesting is how her body is what saves both women. It is her labor in Boaz's field that gets her noticed initially. It is her seduction of Boaz on the threshing floor that causes him to step up to be the redeemer of Naomi and Ruth. It is her fertile womb that produces a child for Naomi. From beginning to end, Ruth uses her body to get what is needed for survival. While many people praise Ruth for her devotion to Naomi, and rightly so, I invite you to think about what is happening in the story: they celebrate the way she perpetuates the people of Israel.

I'm not sure about you, but I know plenty of women who are mothers, but that alone is not what makes them remarkable people. What makes those women remarkable are things such as the way they choose to rear those children to be confident, loving game-changers, themselves. The remarkable women I know are involved in their communities. They run successful businesses. They are elected governmental officials. They are involved in the education of children. They are mindful of the resources of our planet. They are poets and journalists, engineers and teachers, doctors, lawyers, therapists and farmers. They are inspiring to me because they are true to themselves and their own passions. In short, they make a difference in this world beyond the use of their womb.

Laws about Women

Exodus 20–24 is a helpful section to read for this purpose. The "Top Ten," the ten commands found in Exodus 20:1–17, may be familiar, but read them again with women in mind this time. You might be surprised at what you notice.

Not only are women discussed as property, as the final commandment makes clear, but they are also not the intended recipients of these commands. Did you notice that? Contemplate how these two assumptions as starting points will influence everything else said about women in those passages, if not in the rest of the Bible.

Exodus 21:1–6 talks about slaves, specifically addressing the issue of to whom a male slave's wife and children belong. Women and children were property, so were enslaved women and children the property of the male slave or the slaveholder? Exodus 21:7–11 discusses expectations of daughters who are sold into slavery. Knowing how difficult children can be at times, I am sure some of you might have joked with other parents about selling a daughter to the highest bidder. But this passage is discussing very real human trade.

Exodus 22:16–18 shows us the cultural value of a female's virginity. Aside from one reference in Revelation, a male's virginity is never discussed in the Bible. Thus "virgin" will always refer to a female. A virgin would be purchased at a greater price than a young woman who had lost her virginity or had it taken from her.

Think about what the deeper issue would have been behind this way of seeing women. The issue was not that of expecting a woman (but not a man) to wait until being married to have sex. Like it or not, this boils down to an issue of territory and staking claims over a woman's body. To be painfully clear, they saw sex as a way of marking territory rather than it having anything to do with love. I'm not sure which is worse, though, that this is in the Bible or that some people still talk about sex and women this way.

Conclusion

We can read all these passages that tell us that men were more important than women and chalk it all up to reflecting the time and place. We can perhaps joke about the way women were property and that their value was in their ability to produce children. The trouble is that many of these ideas are still at work in our supposedly "enlightened" society, and most notably in communities that have a good deal of "Bible-believing" constituents. Coincidence? I do not think so.

WOMEN CLOSE TO JESUS

Since I already addressed Mary Magdalene and the women who reportedly anoint Jesus, in chapter 6, I'd like to talk here about other women involved in the Gospels. I hope you will take a quick assessment of your thoughts on this topic: Who were the women who were close to Jesus, and what was their role in Jesus' world?

Many people will suggest that Jesus chose to hang out with tax-collectors and prostitutes, so we can say that some of the women "close" to him were sex workers. Yes? Stop to think about what this really would have looked like.

There are other fairly significant women to take note of, however. Luke 8:1–3 tells us that Mary Magdalene and a handful of other women were his "sugar mamas"! However these women came by their wealth, Mary, Joanna, Susanna, and many others were apparently willing to spend it on Jesus and a dozen of his friends. What I love about this tidbit, given its placement at the beginning of Jesus' mission, is that it now allows us to picture or envision women present with Jesus all along his journey. Any story that discusses Jesus and his disciples you can now imagine including a few women as well. Perhaps it would be more honest to say that Jesus had male and female disciples, but due to social constraints at that time, the women were not mentioned in most of the stories.

Then there is the "Mary and Martha" passage (Luke 10:38–42). Mary and Martha are somewhat iconic in church circles. People like to use their names to refer to the contrast between "busybodies" and those who are more contemplative in congregations. "Are you a Mary or a Martha?" people ask. It seems to me that neither description is entirely true to the passage (or fair to women in the church).

The passage tells us that Mary sat listening to Jesus and that Martha was distracted by making dinner and was annoyed that Mary was not helping. A friend offered me a life-changing interpretation of this passage when she told me that it is not simply that Mary chose the better thing, but the very fact *that she chose* was better than giving in to social expectations, as Martha was doing.

Admittedly, this is not the only way to read what Jesus says to Martha, but it is an authentic reading when you look at the Greek in this passage. A word-for-word translation can be phrased either "For Mary chooses the good part" or "For Mary choosing is the good part." For me, and many other people I have met along the way, hearing a message from Jesus affirming that it was okay to be true to myself was one of the most freeing moments in my life. "That she chose"—such a simple concept. The empowerment this concept has granted me and thousands of others is not so simple, however; it is actually rather astonishing.

Finally, consider the women to whom Jesus appeared on resurrection. It may have simply been "women's work" to go anoint bodies for burial, so the fact that it was women who went to the tomb on the third morning is not absolute proof that the women disciples were more devoted to Jesus than his male disciples were. But what does it say to you that when it came to Jesus showing himself to people after his resurrection, he revealed himself to a woman, Mary Magdalene, first? Jesus in the resurrected state: this is the crux of Christian belief. This is an important detail for the Church, and it was revealed to a woman. Hmmm.

PAUL ON WOMEN

At times, I simply feel badly for Paul, because he is rather misunderstood. The take on women presented in the latter portion of the New Testament is much more complex than most people think. I often hear people say that Paul was negative toward women or that he wanted them to be silent in church and definitely not to lead worship. What are your thoughts about Paul's view of women? For those of you quite familiar with his letters, it might also be helpful to note which ones you are drawing on for referencing in light of the following comments. In order to handle this section on Paul adequately, we first have to address two things about Paul's thirteen letters: why he wrote them and who actually wrote them.

The reason Paul wrote letters was to address problems or questions that came up in the communities of Jesus followers that he had established. Please note: he was never present in the town when the problem arose. Someone from the town in question would track him down, tell him what had developed, and Paul and his buddies would collectively write a letter responding to the issue, which would be taken back and read in the meeting. Many people today are a bit shocked to learn about how subjective the whole process was.

On the matter of who wrote Paul's letters: we have good reasons to think that six of his letters were written by other people and just attributed to him. The first time I heard this suggestion, I rejected it outright. My reasoning went something like this: "If the letter opens with 'Paul, an apostle of Christ Jesus . . .' then I trust that it was written by Paul. After all, something in the Bible would not contain a lie or misleading information." As it turns out, however, just because it has Paul's name on it as the sender does not mean that he and his companions actually wrote it.

Before you get uncomfortable or think about skipping this section, you might want to consider the reasons this might happen. For instance, if a new issue arose, after Paul had died, one of the men who knew him well might have tried to address it as he thought Paul would have. Instead of "what would Jesus do?" it was a "what would Paul say?" moment. Though we are not certain when Paul died, a safe bet is the mid-60s, during the Neronian persecution in Rome. Thus, Ephesians, Colossians, 1 and 2 Timothy, and Titus, written after the mid-60s, would all be in this category.

Another possibility is that some of the advice that Paul gave in one of his early letters was taken the wrong way or led to more problems. Either way, someone needed to respond in Paul's voice in order to correct the problem. For instance, compare what 1 and 2 Thessalonians say about "the *parousia,*" Christ's return to earth (1 Thess. 4:13–18; 2 Thess. 2:1–12). In the first letter, Paul indicates that we will have no clue as to when to expect it. It appears that some people heard this and stopped working, because the second letter has a good deal of "get back to work!" kind of content. The second letter also mentions several things that will happen prior to the day arriving, giving them "clues" to look for.

Chart 4: Paul's Words on Women

	Genuine Paul	Disputed Paul
Women in Leadership	Romans 12; 16 1 Corinthians 11:2–16 1 Corinthians 12 1 Corinthians 14:33–36 Galatians 3:28	Ephesians 4:1–16 1 Timothy 2
Leadership Roles in the Church	_____	1 Timothy 3
Dynamic between Husband and Wife	1 Corinthians 7	Ephesians 5:21–33 Colossians 3:18–19

There is also the possibility that someone was banking on Paul's popularity. A letter attributed to Paul would get more immediate attention than one written by some "nobody." This could come from good intentions, by the way. Things were a bit tricky, even dangerous, for people in the Jesus movement at first. Using Paul's name could allow a person safe anonymity.

One of the most striking reasons that we think some of Paul's letters were not by Paul is because of the way certain topics are handled in the early letters ("genuine Pauline" letters) versus in the later letters ("disputed Pauline" letters). Some of these topics, in addition to matters about the *parousia*, are salvation (do we have it now or in the future?), rulers and principalities (human or spiritual rulers), and women in leadership.

The "genuine Pauline" letters are quite affirming of women in whatever role they are gifted to fill. The "disputed Pauline" letters are not. Some people suggest that Paul simply changed his mind on that issue. But part of what we see in the Newer Testament writings is that women's initial involvement in leadership was misunderstood politically. Thus, for political reasons, there was a change in the party line on women's roles in leadership.

Chart 4 above can help you compare for yourself some of the "genuine Paul" and "disputed Paul" discrepancies that relate to women.

Some of the passages in the "Genuine Paul" column need some explanation. I'll address them as they are ordered in the chart.

Romans

Romans 12 and 1 Corinthians 12 are included in this chart in order for you to see that the "genuine" Paul never refers to specific leadership roles in the Church. He simply talks about how people's gifting needs to be used and how the Spirit gives gifts as God sees fit. The issue of a person's sex or gender is not even a part of the conversation in these two chapters.

Romans 16 is in this list because of the comments about Phoebe and the other women mentioned in the greeting (16:1–16). Comparing the label given to Phoebe, in several translations, is rather eye-opening. The Greek word, *diakonos*, is translated with everything from "special servant" to deacon to minister. Does it matter which label you ascribe to Phoebe? Perhaps the answer to that question is found in the associations you make with each option, especially in terms of the power and respect each are given. For many people, serving is the greatest thing a person can do. Thus, calling Phoebe a servant is not considered a put down for her at all.

But look at this from a different angle. Romans is the one letter that Paul wrote to a group without having visited them first. It is something of an introduction of his thought for those who didn't know him, and he was trying to solicit their financial support for his trip to Spain. All this helps to explain why the list of names in the greeting section is so long compared to his other letters.

Regarding Phoebe, then, it is significant that Paul mentions her first and has such high praise for her. He "commends" her to them, which we never see him doing elsewhere. He suggests that when she says, "Jump!" they say, "How high?" She is apparently a wealthy woman, since she funded the travels of many people, including Paul. Add to all this the fact that nowhere else does (the genuine) Paul refer to someone holding a specific role. So whatever you want to call Phoebe, it seems that his intention is to say something important about her and her leadership.

Paul mentions the couple Prisca and Aquila next, though he has atypically listed the female first. Perhaps Prisca was the more outgoing or influential of the two. Whatever the case, he says that they risked their lives for him and that "all the churches of the Gentiles" ought to be grateful to them. Given that Paul's work was focused on the Gentiles, this couple was pretty important to him and to the entire Church. That makes Prisca pretty significant.

The last person I would like to point out is mentioned in 16:7. The name in question is Junia, which is listed as Julia or Junias in other ancient manuscripts. The reason this bit matters is that Junia was a woman's name, Junias a man's. Paul calls Andronicus and Junia(s) "kinsmen and fellow prisoners, who are outstanding among the apostles." Again, those are fairly impressive kudos. But given these two are listed as a couple, it is more likely that this is referencing a woman, Junia.

But I hope you will think about the fact that in copying this letter, some of the scribes changed Junia's name to a man's. Whatever the reason for it, this little incident raised some questions for me when I first learned about it. At that point in time, it wasn't really about me needing a woman to be affirmed. It was that I had believed that scripture was trustworthy, even in the details. To see that someone had changed this detail, and in doing so erased a person's contribution, rattled me to my core. I was realizing, on new levels, that things were not as they had seemed.

What Paul does say about women in Romans 12 and 16 is positive and affirming. This is an important detail to pay attention to.

1 Corinthians

I include 1 Corinthians 7 in the chart because of the way Paul discusses what the dynamics between husbands and wives should look like. He seems to be focused on sex and whether or not one member of a marriage can withhold it from the other. Never mind that Paul was a declared celibate person giving sex advice to couples. The takeaway on this is how shockingly egalitarian his commands are. Add to this the fact that what happens "in the bedroom" is a microcosm of the relationship overall. To be clear, this is the only place in the Bible where a husband and wife are talked about with such thorough and explicit equality.

There are two tricky passages in 1 Corinthians that people turn to on this topic of women in leadership: 11:2–16 and 14:33–36. Let me state up front that I think both passages are affirming the leadership of women in the Church, though most people read them as saying just the opposite. Wild, eh?

The main thing to keep in mind in understanding 1 Corinthians 11:2–16 is that parts of it are someone else's assertions that Paul is quoting in order to counter them. We know that Paul was quite handy with the rhetorical devices, one of which is to quote your opponent in order to indicate where you disagree (a tactic we still use today). Unfortunately, there was no punctuation equivalent to our quotation marks in Paul's day to set off the points Paul is citing, but reading 11:2–16 this way makes this section much easier to understand. Paul's comments/ideas are in normal text and the opponent's comments/ideas are italicized:

> 11:2   I commend you because you remember me in everything and maintain the traditions just as I handed them on to you.

> *11:3–10   But I want you to understand that Christ is the head of every man, and the husband is the head of his wife, and God is the head of Christ. ⁴Any man who prays or prophesies with something on his head disgraces his head, ⁵but any woman who prays or prophesies with her head unveiled disgraces her head—it is one and the same thing as having her head shaved. ⁶For if a woman will not veil herself, then she should cut off her hair; but if it is disgraceful for a woman to have her hair cut off or to be shaved, she should wear a veil. ⁷For a man ought not to have his head veiled, since he is the image and reflection of God; but woman is the reflection of man. ⁸Indeed, man was not made from woman, but woman from man. ⁹Neither was man created for the sake of woman, but woman for the sake of man. ¹⁰For this reason a woman ought to have a symbol of authority on her head, because of the angels.*

> 11:11–12   Nevertheless, in the Lord woman is not independent of man or man independent of woman. ¹²For just as woman came from man, so man comes through woman; but all things come from God.

> *11:13–15   Judge for yourselves: is it proper for a woman to pray to God with her head unveiled? ¹⁴Does not nature itself teach you that if a man wears long hair, it is degrading to him, ¹⁵but if a woman has long hair, it is her glory? For her hair is given to her for a covering.*

> 11:16   But if anyone is disposed to be contentious—we have no such custom, nor do the churches of God.

Marginal Notes Become Scripture?!

The thought of someone revising or adding to what is in scripture is nothing short of heresy for many people. There is, for them, a sacred trust in what the Bible says, even in the details. But the reality of the situation tells us that people did meddle with what was in scripture, both before and after the Newer Testament canon had been set. While we can never know the motivations of the people who added those marginal notes to the manuscripts, we can assume that they were added for clarity or to address an issue that had arisen, and this seemed to be a good place to add the corrective.

There are numerous examples of it, as a comparison of manuscripts shows. Two specific examples are at the beginning of Mark's Gospel and the beginning of Ephesians.

Though Mark's Gospel begins with, "The beginning of the good news of Jesus Christ, son of God," the earliest manuscripts do not have the "son of God" part. This was likely added later, reflecting the early church's need to clarify who Jesus was.

Similarly, we have a manuscript that has the Greek words for "in Ephesus" written in the margin, at the beginning of the letter. This tells us that the letter was written, initially, without the specific recipients named. But since it was added to the margins, the next time that letter was copied "in Ephesus" was incorporated into the body of the letter.

Knowing this information has changed the way many people think about the Bible. It tends to make them see the Bible as less perfect and more human, which is not the worst thing in the world.

Note how in verse 2, Paul commends the people in Corinth for maintaining the traditions he handed on to them. But verse 3 states a belief about husbands and wives that directly counters what Paul says in 1 Corinthians 7, just four chapters earlier. Think about this for a moment. Either Paul is having a psychotic break in the middle of writing this letter, or we ought to read this section with some attention to the rhetorical moves and see the argument through to the end.

Compare 11:8–10 and 11–12. Verses 8–10 seem to be stating one view of men and women and 11–12 a slightly different view. If you read these verses, I think you'll see that it is difficult for one person to be stating all of it as firm conviction. The same can be said of verses 13–15 and 16. This whole section, 11:2–16, is more of a dialogue than a proclamation. This back-and-forth dynamic is driven home in verse 16, when Paul says that he knows of no such custom, nor do the churches of God.

The piece that often gets overlooked in trying to understand this passage is that nowhere in there does Paul or his opponent deny that women can and do lead worship (see vv. 4 and 5). The issue, it seems, is how women should be dressed when they do lead in worship. The fact that scripture makes a big deal of the attire of women but not of men is an issue for another day.

This rhetorical device is used again at the end of 1 Corinthians 14, when an opposing idea is quoted and then refuted. In this case, it probably wasn't Paul himself but a like-minded friend, because these few verses appear to have been added to the letter at some point. Notice how verses 33b–36 (33b means to start with the second half of verse 33) can be removed and the flow of chapter 14 is not disturbed? It is actually a bit smoother. Why don't you try reading 1 Corinthians 14:26–40 without 33b–36 and see what you think. Most likely, these verses were added as a marginal note, which was then incorporated into the body of the letter when it was copied the next time. This is another idea that I initially wanted to reject outright. But we do know that this happened at times (see "Marginal Notes Becoming Scripture?!" above).

It appears that 14:33b–36 was most likely added in response to an opposing idea being professed by others in the early Church and recorded in passages such as 1 Timothy 2:11–12. First Timothy is one of those letters that is attributed to Paul but most likely was not by him and his friends. It seems that someone who knew Paul well heard about the ideas in 1 Timothy 2, knew that this was counter to the way Paul thought about women in the worship setting, and added a summary (vv. 33b–35) and refutation (v. 36) of that idea to a letter genuinely written by Paul. Chart 5 puts these two passages side by side so that you can see what I mean.

The NRSV's use of the word "or" in verse 36 ("Or did the word of God originate with you?") just doesn't capture the outrage the writer seems to be expressing. If you read verses 33b–35 as one opinion and verse 36 as the response to it, then you avoid the awkward acrobatics of making it all flow as one opinion. Additionally, this way of reading 14:33b–36 makes it consistent with the rest of the 1 Corinthians passages that affirm women in leadership. First Corinthians 14:33b–35, while sounding strikingly similar to 1 Timothy 2:11–12, directly contradicts what is said in 1 Corinthians 11 and 12. Additionally, there

Chart 5: Silent in Church?

1 Corinthians 14:33b–36	1 Timothy 2:11–12
As in all the churches of the saints, [34]women should be silent in the churches. For they are not permitted to speak, but should be subordinate, as the law also says. [35]If there is anything they desire to know, let them ask their husbands at home. For it is shameful for a woman to speak in church. [36]What?! Did the word of God originate with you? What?! Are you the only ones it has reached?* *Author's translation on v. 36.*	[11]Let a woman learn in silence with full submission. [12]I permit no woman to teach or to have authority over a man; she is to keep silent.

is no law, yet, that asserts that women should be submissive as 14:34 claims. It is also worth noting that some ancient manuscripts have verses 34 and 35 after 40. At the very least this tells us that this segment was added to the original letter.

How interesting that these two passages, 1 Corinthians 14 and 1 Timothy 2, represent completely opposite beliefs that were alive and well in the early Church, and both perspectives are canonized! Two directly contradictory voices about women in leadership in the Church are right there in the Bible, and they are both attributed to Paul. Hmmm.

Galatians

Galatians 3:28 is one of my favorite verses to discuss on this topic. "There is no longer Jew or Greek, there is no longer slave or free, there is no longer male and female; for all of you are one in Christ Jesus." Given the context of this verse, we know that Paul is addressing how these categories from everyday life should be handled in the meeting of Jesus' followers. While they might respect "Jew and Gentile," "slave and free," "male and female" in everyday encounters, in the space created by Christ, none of those categories are to apply to the way they interact with one another.

Did you catch that? This claim nullifies any suggestion that there are "men's" roles or "women's" roles in the Church. This is a pretty huge claim! If this is what Paul was saying, why do you suppose the Church changed its mind about this equality?

As I mentioned earlier, it seems that part of the reason that the leaders in the Church changed the message about women in leadership is due to their leadership being misunderstood politically. Let me explain.

PAUL AND POLITICS?

I ventured into this "faith and politics" issue in chapter 1: "What About Separation of Church and State?" Here are a couple additional ideas for your consideration regarding the role of politics in the early Jesus movement.

The first is that while the word *church* is primarily a religious term today, the Greek word it is translating, *ekklēsia*, was originally a political term. An *ekklēsia* was a social or political group comprised only of men, often with membership dues, serving various purposes. In ancient Athens, for instance, it was the main assembly of the men who helped make military or economic decisions about the city. Paul's choice to label the meetings of Jesus' followers as an *ekklēsia* should tell us that those gatherings resembled a political or social gathering.

The second point is the connection between stable households and political stability. There was a political or philosophical ideal at the time that said that men were to be the head of their households: the husband to the wife, the master to the slaves, and the father to the children. The reason for this "household code" structure was to ensure that the households were being run and maintained well. A city full of well-run households will be a well-run city. A region full of well-run cities will be stable. The Empire depended on stable regions. So then, as now, the household politics had a direct impact on the politics of the state or Empire.

The way this "household politics" relates to the early Jesus movement, then, is because the gatherings initially took place in homes. Thus, there would have been two sets of gender roles playing out in the same space: when it was "just a home," the male was head or leader of the household. When it was the space created by and for Christ, none of those social or political roles applied (master/slave, Jew/Gentile, male/female). But from the outside, who was to know that there was such a distinction?

If, as their worldview claimed, the political stability of a town depended on men being responsible leaders of their households, but some of the homes in the town appear to have women leaders, wouldn't you be a bit suspicious of those households? Women in leadership in house churches threatened the political ideal of the day. Though it may sound like a stretch, I assure you that women having power over men was threatening to the male ideal of men being in control. There are many ways to label this dynamic. I suggest that you think of it as *patriarchy* (literally, father-rule). Women having some status, and thus power, in a gathering that looked like a social or political group threatened patriarchy, which in turn threatened what men thought of as the only reasonable and responsible way to live. This is the main reason that I think we see a change in what is said about roles within the churches: having women in leadership in the Jesus gatherings was seen from the outside as a threat to political stability.

If you recall, Paul's "genuine" writings endorse equality between husbands and wives, and he makes no distinctions according to gender in terms of giftedness. We start to see the gendered household political norms of the day being referenced in the Newer Testament writings from the end of the first century. The political and philosophical ideal of the male head of the household is imposed on the leadership structure of the church gatherings. The "genuine" Paul message of equality in the *ekklēsia* was displaced by the norms of patriarchy in the "disputed" Pauline letters.

You should also know that some of the followers of Christ were being arrested, interrogated, and some even killed because of the ways people misunderstood them. The issue was not that they worshiped Jesus. They were arrested and thought to be subversive, politically, because they would not also give proper honor to the Emperor. Additionally, Christians were thought to be cannibals, robbers, and people indulging in incest. Not giving honor to the Emperor was perhaps the one legitimate accusation. Incidentally, it is one that 1 Peter and Revelation respond to quite differently.

Again, there is plenty more to say about this. In fact, a good bit of my first book deals with this very issue. If you want to know more on this topic, I suggest that you begin by reading the letter between Pliny and Trajan, dated to approximately 113 CE. The letter mentions some things that Christians were being accused of, some of which are referenced in 1 Peter as things they should not be arrested for.

Ephesians, Colossians, 1 Timothy

Many pastors and scholars do not think that these three letters were written by Paul, rather that they were merely attributed to him. These are three of the "disputed Pauline" letters. Ephesians 5:21–33 is important for this discussion. There are many elements worth addressing in that passage, but for now I will pose three questions and observations and hope you'll explore the text further on your own.

First, is it fair to men or to women to pose the idea in verse 22: "Wives, be subject to your husbands as you are to the Lord"? What I mean by that is that this puts undue pressure on the men to be responsible for everything—it sounds so exhausting to me—and puts women quite literally into a subject position to the one person she should be equal to. For whom is this a fair command? Who benefits from this relational dynamic?

My second observation is about why this is applied to all women, today, when it is seemingly talking to "wives" in context. Have you ever thought about that? There are several passages in the Newer Testament that are addressed to (or are translated as addressed to) wives but that people go right ahead and apply to all women. If the title or role of wife is meaningless, why was it used in the first place? What is the parallel message, then, for single women? (Spoiler alert: there is not one.) The concern I am trying to highlight is that discipleship of Christ is often tied to the sets of ideals addressed to wives and husbands, which makes being married an implied assumption.

My third point is that I ask you to think of this passage in comparison to what Paul says in 1 Corinthians 11:11–12 and 1 Corinthians 7 in terms of the power dynamic of equality that he affirms between a husband and a wife. When you read through Ephesians 5:21–33, you will note that the author literally sets up this hierarchy: God-Christ-husbands-wives. Pastors and scholars will point out that the command to men to love their wives would have been progress, since wives were treated as property. This is referred to as "love patriarchalism": infusing the patriarchal ideal of men ruling with a decent dose of love. But it is still within the framework of the patriarchal ideal.

Colossians 3:18–19 is much shorter than the passage from Ephesians, though it is still worth noting. "Wives, be subject to your husbands, as is fitting in the Lord. Husbands, love your wives and never treat them harshly." Women are to be subject and men are not to be harsh. Hmmm. What happened to Paul's "respect each other" message of 1 Corinthians 7?

Finally, let's talk about 1 Timothy. Let me remind you that all these letters in the Newer Testament were written in response to an issue developing in a faith community. Since the initial issue is not always obvious, it is a good practice to read with an eye toward trying to figure it out. If we skip over to 1 Timothy 2:8–15, one of the juiciest Newer Testament passages for women, pay attention and see what you think the initiating issues were.

In light of 1 Timothy 2:9, many people have suggested that wealthy women were flaunting their jewels, expensive clothing, and fancy hairdos in the weekly meetings, causing some distractions. But does that mean that the women were meant to never wear those things, or just not in worship? This is a similar issue to what we saw about the passage in Ephesians. This command, addressing a specific issue in a specific town during their gathering times, has at times been applied to all women in all places and times. Do you think that's an appropriate extension of this passage?

Also, it is a rather interesting way to handle a situation. You tell women to stop expressing themselves in their appearance, though nothing similar is ever said to men, and then tell the women that it is a godly thing to do. This particular matter of attire and telling women to "fix" issues by the way they dress is a huge one, and it seems to me to be addressing the surface issues, not the deep ones. Think of all the talk today about women supposedly being responsible for men's actions if the way they dress is perceived as provocative or lacking in sufficient modesty.

The most delicate part of this passage deserves most of the discussion:

[11]Let a woman learn in silence with full submission. [12]I permit no woman to teach or to have authority over a man; she is to keep silent. [13]For Adam was formed first, then Eve; [14]and Adam was not deceived, but the woman was deceived and became a transgressor. [15]Yet she will be saved through childbearing, provided they continue in faith and love and holiness, with modesty.

What is the issue that has developed that needs to be addressed or corrected by these ideas? There are plenty of suggestions, and there is no way to have certainty on it. So let me offer three bits for your consideration.

First, the directive for women in 1 Timothy 2:11–12 flies in the face of what Paul says in Romans 12 and 1 Corinthians 12 regarding women and "teaching authority." It is important to come to terms with the fact that there are contradictory commands in scripture and that this passage contradicts other genuine Pauline passages. In this case, I refer you to the "Paul and Politics" discussion, above. Were women teaching and having authority, and outsiders perceived this incorrectly? Was it the content of what the women were teaching that was the problem? If the latter, it is worth asking who got to decide what was "proper" content, at the time.

The summary of the "Adam and Eve" story in 2:13–14 is pretty much what we see in Genesis 2–3. So the author might be referring to that story as the justification for why women are to be silent. It could also be that the author is countering a story that was being taught about Adam and Eve, which he thinks is devastatingly incorrect, by reminding them of what the Genesis story says. There is an ancient version of the Adam and Eve story in which Eve is formed first, instead of Adam, and Adam is the one "deceived." Hmmm.

Finally, according to 1 Timothy 2:15, women are actually saved by childbirth! What?! If you consider having the political issues that I mentioned above weigh in on this conversation, some of these claims start to make a bit more sense. Just as we see in 1 Peter 2–3 some commands to women to be silent and subject to their husbands, even in frightening situations, we see in 1 Timothy 2 commands being made to women that not only silence them but also make them look like good, child-bearing citizens. First Peter and 1 Timothy are responding, in part, to similar political dynamics.

This segment of 1 Timothy 2 is an endorsement of the political ideal of rearing well-behaved children, which Emperor Augustus highlighted when he began to give tax relief to people with children. What if by "saved through childbearing" the author means that they will no longer be seen as politically suspect and subjected to arrests and executions if they are having children and rearing them well? There is a story from the second century, "The Acts of Paul and Thecla," about a woman who rejected the married and motherly state, supposedly in response to Paul's teachings. Her choices were seen as politically subversive, and she was rejected by her family for them. In fact, in the story her own mother suggests that she be burned at the stake to make a statement about how inappropriate her choices were. Thus, it is not a stretch to suggest that we could rephrase 1 Timothy 2:11, 12, 15 like this: "The authorities will stop eyeing you so closely if your women would just be quiet and be subject to their husbands and focus on the childrearing duties."

At the end of the day, all the "genuine" and "disputed" Pauline letters are in the Newer Testament. All of them count as content that people today can draw on, so on some level it might seem pointless to go through all this work in order to see the distinction between these two groups. But there is a method to my madness.

First, now when you hear people say that "Paul was against women," you know that is just not the case. Now you know that there are at least two trajectories in the Newer Testament regarding how women were told they could contribute to the worship setting. The real Paul was quite affirming of women and their giftedness.

Second, I have differentiated between the "genuine" and the "disputed" Paul to highlight that there are at least two trajectories regarding women that have been canonized. Think about that. If you want to turn to the Bible as the final word on how to handle the issue of women in leadership, then you have to make choices regarding which biblical passages to include and which to ignore. To this end, I encourage you to ponder why someone would choose to treat the more restrictive later passages as more authoritative than the earlier ones that give women freedom.

Directives to "Be Silent"

In the previous section, we looked at some of the verses that tell women to learn in silence and that women are not to have authority over men (1 Timothy 2:8–15). This passage also includes the ideas that women were not to braid their hair or wear gold or jewels or fine clothes. Notice how similar that is to 1 Peter 3:1–4, where women's attire is quieted down: they are told to have a "gentle and quiet spirit" and are told to use their actions not words with their husbands. There is a fascinating theme of "silencing women" at work in both passages.

Have you ever thought about what it does to people when you tell them that they cannot express themselves outwardly, through their jewelry, clothing, or hairstyles? For most people, what you wear affects your mind-set. There are reasons that work attire is often more formal and "put together" than everyday clothing. Style magazines are not simply banking on people's desires to be trendy or to fit in but also on the fact that what we put on our bodies affects our view of ourselves and communicates a bit of who we are to those we encounter. When someone in the Bible tells women that they cannot express themselves outwardly, that person is silencing or "shutting down" women's personalities.

We could have a rather long and involved discussion about women not being allowed to teach or have authority over men. But in all honesty, I would prefer to appeal to reason for a moment. Does it make sense for people to be silenced when they have productive things to contribute? Does it make sense to you that God would create people as they are but not want them to use those gifts for the betterment of everyone?

What is usually happening, when people try to control others, is that they are afraid of the power those others have. Fear often drives control. I am fairly certain that fear has no place in a community built on love. I am also certain that constantly requiring women to be subject to men is a social expectation of the time in which these Newer Testament texts were written. This is yet another excellent example of the issue of our cultural norms changing, while the texts being read have not.

Conclusion to Paul on Women

However you sort through what I have offered here, I hope you can see that there is some element of tension in the Pauline letters regarding thoughts about women speaking and leading in worship settings and in terms of the dynamics between husbands and wives. Something significant must have happened to have the approved message from Paul go from "the whole body needs women to use their gifts in church" (Romans 12, 1 Corinthians 12) to "women are to be quiet in church" (1 Timothy 2) and to go from "husbands and wives belong to each other" (1 Corinthians 7:4) to "wives be subject to your husbands" (Ephesians 5:4). Think about it. Permission granted.

CONCLUSION

I would like to circle back around and ask you why you think a person might turn to the Bible for input on how women should behave or how they can be involved in worship settings. First, I think it is important to be thoughtful as to why people do trust the Bible, especially on this topic. Second, I think it is just as important to be thoughtful about why people continue to defer to what is in the Bible related to this topic. These might seem like the same points, but I do not think that they are.

The reasons people do trust the Bible have to do with the way they grew up and the fact that people in their lives valued and trusted the Bible. There is an element of tradition, both within families and in the Church, which makes this respect for the Bible quite understandable. It just so happens that a great deal of what many Christians believe about the nature of husband/wife relationships, or just what a godly woman looks like, is based on what we see in scripture. This is what they were taught and this is what they trust.

The reason that people continue to defer to the Bible regarding this particular topic, I think, is mostly because they have been taught to fear God and respect God's Word as it is. They have specifically been told that they may not challenge something that they find in the Bible.

It truly breaks my heart when I see well-intentioned people upholding or defending "biblical truths" on this topic. Good intentions do not outweigh the harm that has come from being true to what is in scripture. Just because an idea is in the Bible does not mean that it is inherently good or correct or life-giving or helpful. Many people want to believe that scripture is always good and useful, but thousands of people I know can give you additional examples and reasons for why this is not the case.

I think it is time for all people who read the Bible to challenge how scripture depicts women, what it requires of them, and the depth of potential harm engendered toward women by these passages.

 ## TAKE THE BIBLE INTO YOUR OWN HANDS

1. How do you typically think about women of the Bible? What different categories might you put them in? If you are a woman, how does this exercise impact the way you think about yourself?

2. Do you think the Bible's emphasis on women's value and virtue as defined by sex and childbearing still influences people of faith today? What is at stake when we gloss over stories of women using their sexuality to get what they want?

3. If Jesus was affirming a woman's ability to choose how she will be a part of a faith community, how would this impact the way you read passages that limit what a woman can do? How do examples of women leaders like Deborah and Phoebe compare with other statements in the Bible saying women should not be leaders?

4. How should we read the letters attributed to Paul when their content is contradictory? Is there one biblical perspective on women that trumps the others for you?

5. Does the idea of keeping women silent or subordinate for the sake of being more culturally acceptable in the Roman world change the way you read Newer Testament texts about women in the early Church? How should we read these texts today?

8

Born of a Virgin?

As the name of this chapter indicates, the belief in a virgin birth is one that might surprise you to learn more about. Many people consider it heretical to suggest that it was not meant to be taken as referring to a literal biological miracle. The topic is such an important component of many people's belief systems that challenging it, in any way, feels like too much to bear. In fact, there was a biblical scholar, Jane Schaberg, who wrote a book called *The Illegitimacy of Jesus: A Feminist Theological Interpretation of the Infancy Narratives*. The response to her book indicates how threatening this kind of pursuit can be for some people: some of her property was damaged or destroyed, the Catholic institution where she had tenure at the time threatened to fire her, and she even received death threats. While I might not have sent threatening e-mails to my professor, I do recall how scary this idea was for me to consider initially. But I happen to believe in people's ability to wrestle with this kind of significant topic and be able to come out stronger rather than be defeated by it. Remember, we're going for "the mark of an educated mind" here.

There are three components of this conversation, as I see it. The first is to see where it is used in the Gospels and the Hebrew Bible passages they draw on. The second part is to talk about how the idea of a virgin birth was used in many ancient stories about important or influential people. The final component is to look at how this doctrine of Christian belief developed and some of the ways it plays out for people today.

COMPARISON OF ISAIAH 7:14 AND MATTHEW 1:23

The story of Jesus' birth can be found in two of the four Gospels, in Matthew 1–2 and Luke 1–2. Of these extended stories, the pieces that discuss the miracle of his conception are quite short, which tells us that there are other important parts of the birth stories that the Gospel writers wanted us to know. I hope you will take a few moments to read Matthew 1:18–23 and Luke 1:26–38, if not also the surrounding verses. As you do so, I hope you will pay attention to who it is that receives the message from God about Mary's pregnancy, as well as how the conception will happen.

One of the many themes in Matthew's Gospel is a focus on righteousness, which Joseph is depicted as embodying in the way he handles this surprise pregnancy. Matthew's Gospel also draws on passages from the Hebrew Bible quite often in order to show that the events in Jesus' life can be interpreted as "fulfilling" the scriptures of his tradition. Contrary to popular Christian belief, which is that all these passages in the Hebrew Bible were predicting Jesus and his life, what Matthew does with the quotations is show that Jesus' life events add meaning to, or "fill up," those passages with more meaning.

You will see the lead in: "This happened in order to fulfill what was spoken by the prophet," followed by a quotation from one of the biblical prophets. For instance, Matthew 1:22–23 gives us one of these "fulfillment citations," as they are called.

All this took place to fulfill what had been spoken by the Lord through the prophet:

"Look, the virgin shall conceive and bear a son,
and they shall name him Emmanuel,"

which means, "God is with us."

The way this passage from Isaiah is presented does imply that a virgin will get pregnant, though as many people have pointed out, that does not mean that it didn't happen in the regular way: that a virgin has sex and gets pregnant. But even if we take this announcement to imply that God is the one who impregnates Mary, you still might want to consider the context and translation of Isaiah 7:14, the verse quoted here in Matthew.

It helps to look at the whole chapter in order to have a clear understanding of what is being said in 7:14. The beginning of Isaiah 7 is chock full of names and places, which can be tricky to follow. The main idea is that King Ahaz, king of Judah, had neighbors and relatives who were trying to band together to overtake him and his region. The prophet Isaiah is sent by the LORD to tell Ahaz not to be afraid, and the reason is contained in Isaiah 7:7–8. Essentially, this is a "prediction" that the two groups of people conspiring against Ahaz would soon themselves be overthrown. I say "prediction" because a person could read the political landscape and assess that this was about to happen.

In order for Ahaz to trust that this is, indeed, what was going to happen, the LORD gave Ahaz a sign. The sign itself is described in 7:14–25. You might want to read it for yourself. Essentially, the prophet tells Ahaz that there is a woman Ahaz knows of who is already pregnant, and by the time her child is ten years old the people conspiring against him will be conquered by Assyria. That is the message or the sign. Notice that the woman is not called *a virgin*: "Look, the *young woman* is with child and shall bear a son, and shall name him Immanuel" (italics added). In Isaiah, it is not a miraculous event but an ordinary one.

So you might be wondering how Matthew got the idea to say "virgin" instead of "young woman." In short, it is a matter of something being lost, or gained, in translation!

The short version of the translation issue is that while there is a Hebrew word (*bitulah*) to use when the woman's virginity is important to note, Isaiah 7:14 uses a different one (*almah*), which simply refers to a young woman or maiden. The catch is that these two words were translated into Greek by using the same Greek word (*parthenos*). The author of Matthew would most likely have been using a Greek version of the Hebrew scriptures (the *Septuagint*) and the main manuscripts of Matthew that translation committees use today are in Greek. Thus, when Matthew quotes Isaiah 7:14, we should expect to see *parthenos*, which can genuinely be translated as either "virgin" or "young woman." Perhaps the question we should be asking is why committees consistently choose the former over the latter.

This suggestion leads us to the next aspect of the belief in a virgin birth, which is to take a quick overview of the use of it in ancient traditions and myths.

HISTORICAL SIGNIFICANCE OF "BORN OF A VIRGIN"

I have to tell you that it was quite unsettling, for me, to learn that Jesus was not the first or only person throughout history whom others claimed was born from a virgin. My knee-jerk reaction, and that of many people I know, was to say, "Well, it might have been claimed to have happened to others, but it actually did happen with Jesus." For whatever reason, many Christians have a belief that everything about Christianity is unique to it. In other words, there is no aspect of Christianity that other religions could share, or if they do, it is in a way that is misguided or not fully on the right track. I think it is important to keep in mind that this is part of the way many people learn about their faith traditions.

The reality of the situation is that many important people throughout ancient history were claimed to have had a virgin birth. This list of super-humans or god-like people includes, but is not limited to, Krishna (of Hindu traditions), the Buddha, Zoroaster (ancient Persia), Mithras (India and ancient Persia), and Horus (Egyptian), as well as a plethora of figures in Greek, Aztec, and Japanese mythology and a notable number of kings or rulers. Some people suggest that biblical figures such as Isaac, Samson, Samuel, and John the Baptist belong on the list, given that their mothers miraculously conceived in their old age or after special prayers to God. In Homer's *Iliad*, you will notice that men whose paternity was previously unknown, who did something particularly heroic in battle, would all of a sudden be hailed as a son of a god. The idea was that that kind of selfless and heroic action could have come only from a person of godly parentage. Finally, an early development in the Christian movement lead to a story (*Protevangelium of James*) explaining that Mary's mother, Anna, conceived her in an extraordinary, if not miraculous, way.

What all this tells us is that this idea, in general, meant something to people. Instead of focusing on whether or not it was possible, I'd ask that you direct your attention to what this belief was saying about the person in question. Making this claim communicates that this person will be special or important in significant, even super-human ways.

These are important bits to keep in mind when you read the Gospels contained in the Bible. The birth narratives of Matthew and Luke directly relate to the larger picture that each is trying to paint in terms of who Jesus was (see chap. 9). They both suggest that Jesus had an auspicious birth or first few years. But Mark's Gospel, the one written down first of the four, does not have a birth narrative at all, and the phrase "son of God" at the very beginning of Mark is not present in all ancient manuscripts.

If it sounds as if I am accusing these authors of completely fabricating parts of their stories, take a deep breath. What is important to keep in mind here, as I will address in the next chapter, is that the authors of the Gospels were not trying to recount history accurately. They were trying to communicate something about Jesus, and they used various literary techniques to do so.

What is important here is that some people within the Christian tradition have taken an ancient storytelling meme and believed it as fact instead of as intended, which was to communicate something special about Jesus. The fact that the Church has focused on and run with the virginal aspect of this idea is what I invite you to think about next.

MARY: VIRGIN AND MOTHER?

In this final section of the chapter, let's think about three things. The first is the reason for the belief in the virgin birth—it might surprise you! The second is what this belief does to the way people see Mary, since they talk about her as a virgin and the mother of Jesus simultaneously. Finally, this belief has led to some ideas about purity and sex, and even how to view women, that are quite powerful and that continue to affect us to this day.

For most Roman Catholics and Orthodox Christians, this idea of Mary as virginal mother is a central component of faith and ritual—as is the belief in her perpetual virginity (that is, that she never had sex in her entire life), which also led to the idea of Mary's Immaculate Conception. For many Protestants, Mary as virginal mother is also a component believed in, though it is not usually front and center in worship services, prayers, or devotional moments.

To be clear: "born of a virgin" is central to the doctrine of the Church, as noted in the creeds. For this reason, most Christians simply accept and affirm it as truth. For those who embrace it as something that literally happened, it is usually explained by saying that "with God, anything is possible." This phrase allows a person of faith to understand the biological necessity of needing two humans to create a baby, but since Jesus was special, even unique, it was possible that God broke the rules of biology in Jesus' conception.

Reason for "Virgin Birth"

For just a few moments, though, I invite you to pause and think about the reasons for this doctrine, with no judgment on what you might think, say, ask, or conclude in response. We have seen some of the historical context for this idea. You might be surprised to see how the Church wrestled with and applied this belief.

Ultimately, in the doctrine of the Church, Jesus' crucifixion is interpreted as a sacrifice for the sins of humanity. The only way this could work, according to the sacrificial system of the Jews (discussed in chap. 5), was if Jesus was pure and blameless and sinless. The only way to have a human born without sin was to leave sex out of the equation, or so the thinking goes.

As discussed, briefly, in chapter 3, some men in the early Church connected the belief in "original sin" to sex. They imported into Genesis 3 the idea that Eve convinced Adam to eat some of the fruit by seducing him first. In this way, they thought of Eve as a sexual temptress and sex as what led to the "original sin" of disobedience. As noted before, there are several pieces of these claims that are simply not supported by the Genesis story. Thus, this conviction that sex is intimately connected to sin came from the Church Fathers, not from scripture.

Furthermore, the Church Fathers claimed that in Adam, all people have sinned. The thinking is that because Adam sinned, and we are all (theoretically) his descendants, we have all inherited this sin issue. Their claim was that sex is the means through which sinfulness is passed along from one generation to the next, so sex itself is seen as sinful.

Let's put these pieces together. Jesus' execution is seen as the ultimate sacrifice for sins. Jesus, thus, had to be pure and blameless, as a sacrificial animal had to be. Any child conceived in the regular way would be sinful. Thus, Jesus' conception by God and a virginal Mary became necessary in Christian thinking.

Mary as Virgin and Mother

Biblical scholars and theologians alike have weighed in on some of the implications or logical conclusions that people have made based on calling Mary both a virgin and a mother. Many of their comments are too long or complicated to unpack here. But think about this combination for a moment. Mary is simultaneously held up as an example because of her "pure" state as virgin and unquestionably as a mother. She embodies an impossible combination. She is the great exception.

Consider what this contributor to *The Women's Bible* said at the end of the nineteenth century: "I think that the doctrine of the Virgin Birth as something higher, sweeter, nobler than ordinary motherhood is a slur on all the natural motherhood of the world." Even if you do not agree with the statement, can you see her point? Is your motherhood, or that of your own mother, friends, or sisters, less noble because it originated with sex?

It is also worth your thoughtfulness that Mary as virgin and mother is depicted primarily as passive or willingly receptive, and she is celebrated in her passivity. Mary as Virgin, for many people, represents the feminine dimension of the divine, but this has never been used to promote the equality of women with men. Rather, idealizing the female in this way is done to compensate for actual social position. Consider these two points: 1) In countries with a strong focus on Mary in the Church, the women are not significantly involved in public and political life. 2) In churches with the strongest attachment to Mary, women are most strongly denied full participation. Hmmm.

The honoring of Mary as Virgin mother is the epitome of male "awe and reverence," even though in doing so, they are putting Mary on a pedestal. What is fascinating to me is how often I have seen this kind of dynamic play out in relationships today. The man in a relationship says that the woman is so valuable or so important that he wants to take care of everything for her. But in doing so, he makes her a kept woman, not one who is empowered. She is often treated as if she would break if touched instead of being seen for the strong and capable woman that she is. When a female is placed on a pedestal, this is actually a form of control, of keeping her in "her place." What is supposed to reflect respect for the woman is instead a form of oppressing or repressing her.

Continuing Effects of This Belief

Can you imagine what these ideas end up communicating to people, however unintentionally, about sex and our bodies? Or about the roles of women and their sexuality?

With this perspective in mind, any natural sexual desires you have are automatically deemed sinful. Think about that: the act that leads to perpetuating the human race is deemed sinful! No wonder so many people have issues embracing the joy and pleasure of sex, when these tapes are playing in the background of their minds. It does not take a theologian to figure out that this is also saying something negative about our bodies, in general, given the role they play in sexual intercourse.

Furthermore, it is not just that sex is equated with sinfulness, in that sex makes a person impure, based on body parts coming together. When a man penetrates a woman, he makes her dirty. She is no longer "pure." While the focus is always on the woman and her lack of purity, as a result of sexual intercourse, it is accomplished by the male's penis and by his act of entering her and the subsequent bodily fluids exchanged. Body parts and fluids are, apparently, dirty and sinful. Really?

Additionally, for many women in the Church, and perhaps in other realms that are influenced by similar ideals of sex and purity, there is a fascinating mixed message in Mary's story. Mary does not express her sexuality, but she is a vessel for a child. This sends a message that making babies is an important role, but being "sexually pure" is also important. Enjoying sex is nowhere in this picture. More than one person has bemoaned the bizarre double standard here in terms of how often sexuality for women is discussed negatively but for men is affirmed.

There is also the vexing "madonna/whore" complex, which implies that a woman is one extreme or the other. Both *virgin* and *whore* are about a woman's sexual experience, or lack thereof, with men. Thus, even this overly simplistic dualism says more about the role men have had in a woman's life than about the woman herself. Fascinating, isn't it? Do you suppose this belief in the virgin birth plays any role in such views?

Given all the harm that repressing sexual desire, unnecessarily, has led to, it seems to me that it is time to talk more reasonably about bodies and sex. Instead of respecting the power of sex, many Christian traditions today try to scare people away from sex by labeling it as something terrible. Even children pick up on the sex-is-bad rhetoric and will pronounce it in college classrooms as young adults, without skipping a beat, even while participating in it on a regular basis. Think of the dissonance they live with unnecessarily.

CONCLUSION

If nothing else, I hope you have a glimpse into how complex the doctrine of the virgin birth actually is. There is a great deal on the line, theologically speaking, when this belief is challenged. Thus, we ought to engage in this conversation carefully and respectfully. At the same time, given the detrimental impact this belief has had on ideas about our bodies and our sexualities, I think we owe it to ourselves and our children to honestly confront this conversation and question the helpfulness of this doctrinal belief.

 **TAKE THE BIBLE INTO YOUR OWN HANDS**

1. What is your understanding of the idea of the virgin birth and its importance for your faith?

2. How does the fact that the Isaiah passage that Matthew 1:23 quotes uses "young woman" instead of "virgin" in the Hebrew affect your reading of the text?

3. Were you aware that other important ancient figures were also claimed to have been born of a virgin? How does this impact the way you see or think of Jesus' birth?

4. Why do you think Mary's virginity (or even more significantly, her mother's virginity) is so essential to many Christians? What do you think of the focus on sexual purity in both biblical stories and theological ideas and of how it is applied to men and women today?

5. What importance does Mary have in your faith? Do you think the reverence many Christians have for her is empowering for women or setting an impossible standard?

9

Will the Real Jesus Please Stand Up?

How many times have you heard someone say that he "loves Jesus"? Have you ever heard someone say that she is trying to share "the gospel" or talk about "salvation," as if there is one singular idea about these matters? You might ask these people to tell you what they mean by these words. It can be startling for people to discover that there is more than one "version" of Jesus in the Bible and more than one way of understanding salvation.

I certainly was not aware of these things until someone helped me to sort through the Gospels, each on their own terms. Up to that point, I would quote lines from one Gospel then another, as if finding a theme in two passages meant that they were meant to be read together. In doing so, I was missing the overall message of each of the Gospels. All four of the Gospel writers in the Newer Testament had a specific point they were trying to make about Jesus—points I was missing by not reading each on its own terms.

The discussions in this chapter have to do with understanding ancient biographies, since their authors had different goals than biographers do today, and getting a basic grasp on the depiction of Jesus in each of the four Gospels.

BIOGRAPHIES: THEN AND NOW

Take a moment to think of all the things you might expect to find in a modern biography. Such a list might include the person's birthdate and place, family makeup, socioeconomic status, childhood influences, education, achievements, even "juicy" stories about the person, and so forth. We tend to expect to find every detail that the biographer could give us, as well as some sense of chronology. We would be surprised to find blatant "spin" or content that was not actually attributable to the person in question. This would constitute a lie, from our perspective, or just bad research.

Ancient biographies, however, were not written to satisfy the reader's craving for every detail of a person's life. They were not trying to trace the development of a person's life, nor did they need to be chronologically sound. Ancient biographies were geared toward highlighting and depicting some specific character trait or essence of the person. A biographer pulled together all moments, quips, or interactions of this person that would support the character trait the biographer was going for, leaving out any that were not useful to this end.

There would even be some room to include outright fiction if it was in tune with the character trait the biographer was highlighting. Consider that story about George Washington, as a boy, admitting to chopping down the cherry tree. It is pure fabrication, yet since it communicates that the first president of the United States was an "honest soul," people continue to tell that story.

When it comes to reading the four Gospels, you are perhaps better served thinking of them as versions of ancient biographies than as literal accounts of Jesus' life. Think about what this means for how to read them. You should not expect them to be chronologically sound. Instead of thinking of every story as having transpired exactly as it is narrated, it is more appropriate to think of the various stories that are woven together as serving to point to the "essence" or character of Jesus, according to each Gospel writer. Matthew and Luke's dramatically different birth narratives, for instance, point directly to the "essence" of Jesus in each. For this reason, we miss part of the point when we try to blend their birth narratives together. Take these insights into ancient biographies with you as you look at the essence of Jesus portrayed in each Gospel. But before launching into them, there are four tidbits about the Gospels that you might want to keep in mind.

GENERAL GOSPEL "NEED-TO-KNOWS"

First, consider the order in which we think they were written. Most scholars assume that Mark was written in the mid- to late-60s, Matthew in the late 70s to early 80s, Luke in the 80s, and John in the mid 90s. Matthew comes first in the Newer Testment simply because at the time the Bible as we know it was organized they thought Matthew was written first.

Second, think about what it means that Mark was not written down until sometime in the 60s, which would have been thirty years after Jesus' execution and resurrection. Most of what Mark included would have been passed down to him by word of mouth, though he might have been working with some written sources. Either way, it is good to be honest about what can happen to a story over time.

Third, when I refer to "sources," I am not trying to be dismissive of the importance of the content of the Gospels. There were many written and oral accounts of Jesus floating around in the first century, and all four Gospel writers were working with more than one source for the content they chose to include. We know a great deal about these sources as well. For now, let me say that the first three—Matthew, Mark, and Luke—tend to be discussed together because of the great number of similarities they share. They follow the same basic outline and use many of the same examples and interactions as a part of telling Jesus' story. We refer to these three as the "Synoptic Gospels," because they can be viewed together (syn + optic). John's Gospel is truly in a league all its own.

Finally, we unfortunately do not know who wrote any of the Gospels. The names that we associate with each Gospel were added to them, based on guesses made by the men of the early Church. For instance, the first Gospel is interested in Jewish traditions and scriptures, which is something we might associate with Jesus' disciple, Matthew, who was a tax collector. The other three Gospels were named in similar ways. "Luke" was a Gentile, and the Gospel of Luke is geared toward a Gentile audience. You get the idea. For simplicity's sake, however, I will refer to the author of Mark as "Mark," and so forth.

Keep the goal of ancient biographies in mind as we explore the essential aspect of Jesus that each Gospel is trying to communicate. You should also know that I have not made up these labels for the "essences" of Jesus. They come from Bart Ehrman's *Introduction to the New Testament*.

MARK

One of the great things about talking about Mark first is that it also happens to be the shortest of the four Gospels. That makes it easy to read in one or two sittings, which I highly recommend if you're really into this conversation. People who read through Mark without pausing to mull over a line or passage are often pleasantly surprised by what they hear or see, things they had previously missed when reading one passage at a time. There are also audio forms of the Bible online, if you prefer listening to reading.

The "essence" of Jesus in Mark's Gospel is that he was a misunderstood, suffering Son of God. You might be thinking, "Yes. I already knew that." But I wonder if your understanding of "Son of God" is the same as what they meant by this label in the first century.

First, it is important to keep in mind that Jesus was not the first or only person who has been called "Son of God." In fact, many labels ascribed to Jesus, such as "Savior," "Light of the World," "God of Gods," "King of Kings," "Lord," and "Prince of Peace," were applied to other men or gods prior to Jesus. It may be unsettling to hear that these terms were not unique to Jesus, but it is helpful to have some context and perspective on this title. "Son of God" was applied to many men, but especially to the emperors of Rome, beginning with Augustus (Octavian). Other examples include many of the kings in the Ancient Near East and kings of Israel, as well as Egyptian pharaohs. It is a title given to the person who was to sit on David's throne. Even in the Psalms we see God claiming David or the psalmist as "son" (2:7; 110:3), perhaps a precursor to that "we are all God's children" kind of idea. Sometimes, in the Hebrew Bible, it refers to angel- or spiritual-type beings (Gen. 6:1–4; Job 1:6).

Additionally, people usually assume that this label, "Son of God," is applied to a God/god. As the examples of it from history indicate, however, this is not the case. "Son of God" often gets confused with "Son of Man," in particular because they are both ascribed to Jesus. Chart 6 is intended to help you sort through what these two labels or roles initially meant.

For those of you still curious about these two labels, I am confident that you will do some research on your own. I would encourage you to go to sources other than Wikipedia or similar websites on this content. I recommend the *Anchor Bible Dictionary*, which is a much more balanced and informed place to begin.

Given that the title "Son of God" ascribed to Jesus meant that he was a special human, why was he misunderstood? It helps to keep in mind that whatever he said or did, he did as a Jew. Jesus would have had the Jewish scriptures in mind and the history of the Jewish people

Chart 6: Son of God vs. Son of Man

Son of God	Son of Man
refers to a special human with god-like qualities	refers to a God who has taken on human form
was applied to many men to indicate their importance, their connection to a God, or that God was "on their side"	ought to be thought of as a role or label—in Daniel it appears to be a role that will be fulfilled; it is not used as a reference to a specific person
Jesus never claims this title; it is ascribed to him	Jesus never claims this title outright but does imply that it applies to himself a time or two

as his foundation. I cannot overstate these points. The way to make sense of why he was misunderstood is to try to be clear on who the Jews were looking for or expecting.

The Jews' expectations stem from the promises given to Abraham in Genesis 12: land, numerous descendants, and to be established enough to be able to help other countries. However, beginning with their story in about 1800 BCE up until the time of Jesus in the first century CE, there is never a time when all three promises were fulfilled, primarily due to foreign powers ruling over them. The role of *messiah*—which means "anointed one," someone literally anointed with oil as an indication of being called to an important role—was a reference to some person who would lead the Jews to a place where the promises could be fulfilled. They needed someone to throw off the rule of a foreign power, in order to be their own people.

From this perspective, you can see why Jesus might be misunderstood. After all, he did not overturn the Roman Empire, or even throw the Romans out of Palestine. They killed him before that could happen. The initial news about this guy Jesus, who was upset about the way his own leadership and the Romans were taking advantage of his people, could have been quite welcome. When interpreted through the lens of a messiah, people might have been excited about him leading a grass roots movement to overthrow the corrupt rulers. But since this is not how things turned out, he would no longer be seen by the Jews as a messiah or Son of God.

This is where Mark's depiction of Jesus is something to grapple with: Jesus was not a messiah or Son of God like the Jews were expecting, yet he is still called Son of God.

Scholars have called this aspect of Mark the "messianic secret" (for some examples, see 1:23–25; 3:7–12; 7:31–37; 8:22–26, 27–30). If Jesus knew that he was a messiah, it seems as if he would have claimed it from the beginning. But this is not what we see happening in Mark. Instead, Jesus consistently tells those "in the know" to keep quiet about it. Hmmm. It is as if he wanted the full story to play out first, since he turns out to embody a new form of being a messiah or Son of God. Jesus turns out to be a Son of God who suffers, who dies, and who is raised from the dead. This is not what the Jews had expected.

Jesus, depicted as the misunderstood, suffering Son of God, communicated, initially, that he was an important human who was a different kind of messiah than the Jews had anticipated. If you read through Mark, I would also encourage you to see any of Jesus' interactions with Jewish leaders as more about power and politics than about whether the leaders believe in him.

MATTHEW

Matthew's portrayal of Jesus is quite different from Mark's in one overarching way. Matthew's Jesus is depicted as being the Jewish Messiah (in contrast to Mark's depiction of Jesus as a kind of a messiah that the Jews had not been anticipating). What you see in Matthew is a portrayal of Jesus as intimately connected to the people, traditions, and scriptures of the Jews. Matthew uses several compelling tactics to convince the reader of Jesus' importance and his role as Jewish Messiah. Most notably, Matthew tells Jesus' story as a kind of parallel to Moses' story, quotes the Hebrew Bible scriptures numerous times to back up his points, and consistently highlights righteousness and Jesus' affirmation or teaching of the law.

Parallel to Moses

There are many ways that we can see parallels between the story of Moses in Exodus and the story of Jesus as depicted in Matthew. Perhaps this parallel was a coincidence. But in light of the way biographies functioned in the ancient world, these parallels suggest an intentional and very strategic move on Matthew's part, capitalizing on the role of Moses to show how significant Jesus was. The suggestion that something said about Jesus in the Gospels might be made up can be offensive to some people. But why not take a look at some of the parallels and decide for yourself what to do with it all?

First, there are similarities in their birth narratives and their connections to Egypt. Both of their lives are directly threatened by a ruler who has children two years old and younger killed (Exod. 1:15–22; Matt. 2:1–12, 16). Moses' ultimate role was to lead the Israelite people out of Egypt. Jesus' story includes being called out of Egypt (Matt. 2:13–15, 19–23).

There is a parallel between these two in terms of the law and the giving of the commandments to the people. Moses goes up a mountain in order to receive the law and commandments. Jesus delivers an interpretation of parts of that Law on a mountaintop, the "Sermon on the Mount" in Matthew 5–7. The first five books of the Bible are traditionally attributed to Moses, regardless of his role in actually writing them. Believe it or not, we can break down Matthew into five different sections, each of which has a speech, followed by related narrative (speech sections: 5–7; 10:16–42; 13; 18; 23–25). Finally, Moses is the giver of the Law to the people. Jesus, throughout Matthew's Gospel, speaks of how to interpret the law and is depicted keeping the law and fulfilling the prophets.

As you deliberate over these parallels, keep in mind that the point was to depict the essence of Jesus for a particular audience. A little creative flair would not necessarily have been seen as deceptive but rather as an important element of ancient biographies.

Other Tactics Used

There are several other aspects of Matthew's Gospel that go a long way toward depicting Jesus as the Jewish Messiah. The most striking, in my opinion, is what we call the fulfillment citations. There are at least eighteen of these (for example, 1:22, 2:15, 2:23, 5:17, 8:17, 12:17, 13:5, 22:4, 27:9). You will see something along the lines of, "this took place to fulfill what was spoken by the prophet," followed by a quotation from a biblical prophet. As I mentioned in chapter 8, many Christians read these passages in Matthew as if the prophet had been predicting this moment in Jesus' life. But I do not think that this is what Matthew intended us to take from these fulfillment citations.

Remember, the prophets spoke and wrote to the people of Israel about what was happening to them at that time. Instead of reading these passages in Matthew as the moment the prophets' words were finally fulfilled, think of them as showing that Jesus was so in tune with

---

The Genealogies in Matthew and Luke

If you're like a lot of people, your eyes just glaze over when you come to a long list of genealogy in the Bible. But genealogies such as those in Matthew's and Luke's Gospels actually have a lot to show us, either by comparing them or by discussing who is in them. They both relate directly to the "essence" of Jesus in each Gospel.

Take a few moments to read through them, looking for similarities and differences between them (Matthew 1:1–7; Luke 3:23–38).

Let me highlight some bits to look for and consider. First, there are the number and names of ancestors. Luke lists fifty-seven generations from Jesus back to Abraham and another twenty-one before Abraham. Matthew lists forty-one generations, starting with Abraham and working down to Jesus. Hmmm. Either Luke added names or Matthew left some out. Also, many of the names that should match up do not! But you do not need to be thrown by this if you keep in mind the purpose of ancient biographies. Luke and Matthew crafted their genealogies to point to their essence of Jesus.

The starting and ending point of each genealogy also tells us something. Since Matthew is trying to emphasize the Jewishness of Jesus, it makes sense that his genealogy would begin with the Father of the Jews, Abraham. Since Luke's essence of Jesus is that he was the Savior of the World, not just of the Jews, it is not a surprise that his genealogy goes all the way back to the "first" generation, Adam, indicating how Jesus is connected to all people.

Many people wonder why Jesus' ancestry is traced through Joseph at all, since Jesus' father is supposed to be God. Yes, if you think of Jesus' birth as a true miraculous event, then God is his father and the genealogy is pointless. If, however, you focus on the fact that Joseph was "righteous"—an important trait in Matthew's Gospel—because he took Mary and her child in, then it is not so pointless. You can also read the "of the Holy Spirit" line in Luke as an indication that this pregnancy is something that God has blessed, regardless of who impregnated Mary.

Also pay attention to the four women specifically mentioned in Matthew: Tamar, Rahab, Ruth, and "the wife of Uriah" (Bathsheba). In addition to all being foreigners, they were all involved in some sort of sex scandal.

Tamar (Gen. 38, a different Tamar from David's daughter in 2 Sam.) is neglected by her father-in-law. After losing two husbands, she should have been married to the third son in the family but is not. She forces her father-in-law to step up, perhaps by rather questionable means (not that she had reasonable alternatives).

Rahab (Josh. 2) protects the spies sent to check out Jericho. Some suggest that she was the madam of the brothel that the two men checked into. (Before you judge her occupation, keep in mind that men kept her in business.) Rahab and her family are spared when the Israelites conquer Jericho.

Ruth's story gets spicy when Naomi pimps her out to Boaz in order to secure his good will on their behalf (Ruth 3). Notice that Ruth is primped and coached on what to do. There is some form of sexual encounter between Boaz and Ruth on the threshing floor, and she leaves early in the morning with "payment" in grain.

The story of "the wife of Uriah" is a drawn-out sex scandal (2 Sam. 11–12), as discussed in chapter 6.

In all four stories, God made something good out of the situations. Perhaps it was for this reason that Matthew included them: if the birth of Jesus had, in one way or another, the whiff of a sex scandal, those women's stories might assure the reader that all will be well.

his people and tradition that even his life events looked similar to the events of his ancestors. In this way, the "fulfilling" of those passages from the Prophets is more like an "adding more meaning" to them than a prediction finally lived out.

It is also worth noting that some of the "fulfilling" moments are a bit of a stretch. For example, in Matthew's depiction of Jesus' entry into Jerusalem (21:1–7), Jesus is supposedly straddling two animals. Hmmm. Matthew is drawing on Zechariah 9:9, which uses poetic verse to announce a king's entrance into Jerusalem. Here, Zechariah employs a literary device we call parallelism. An idea is stated and then repeated for emphasis, sometimes slightly differently, as in Zechariah 9:9: "riding on a donkey, on a colt, the foal of a donkey." Apparently, Matthew was unaware of the parallelism literary device and read Zechariah as referring to two animals. (Compare with Mark 11:4–7; Luke

19:32–35; John 12:14.) Whatever the case, this example tips the hat to the fact that Matthew was using his creative license to ensure that parts of Jesus' story echoed events from the sacred writings of the Jews. Counting these fulfillment citations, there are fifty-three direct quotations from the Hebrew Bible, and seventy-six other references to scripture or other ancient writings in Matthew's Gospel.

There is also a good deal of talk about Jesus, or those affiliated with him, being righteous or fulfilling righteousness. Being righteous is an important aspect of keeping the covenant, as a Jew, as is keeping the law. Jesus is always depicted as upholding the law, if not interpreting it in a new way.

All these components add up to Jesus being fully rooted in his tradition and a continuation, not a replacement, of it. If you were to think of Matthew's Gospel in terms of where it falls in the development of the Christian movement, this essence of Jesus might make a little more sense. The segment of Jews who were Jesus' followers would have stood out as a separate sect of Judaism, initially, since they believed that Jesus was an unexpected form of messiah. The members of other Jewish sects who had not "gotten on board" with this way of seeing Jesus as the Messiah would most likely have been the intended audience of Matthew's Gospel.

This is why Matthew includes numerous references to the scriptures of the Jews, Jesus "fulfilling" these scriptures, Jesus upholding or interpreting the law, Jesus fulfilling the law, and Jesus' own story paralleling that of Moses. Moses, the original giver of the Law, is paralleled in Jesus, who validates and interprets that same Law. Moses, sent to set God's people free, is paralleled by Jesus, who has come to do the same, though this time in a spiritual sense more than a physical sense.

LUKE

Just as I suggested that you try to think of Matthew in terms of its role in the development of the Christian movement, please continue to do so for Luke. Written in the mid 80s, Luke's portrayal of Jesus is as Savior of the World. It reflects some of the development in thought that Paul set in motion some thirty years earlier. Though "Savior of the World" might seem obvious today, when most Christians around the world are not descended from ancient Jews, initially this idea would not have been so clear. When Paul claimed that the Gentiles are now allowed into the covenant that the Jews had with God, through Jesus' death and resurrection, he made a rather bold and unexpected claim. We see Luke applying this idea by depicting Jesus as someone who came to seek and to save the lost, regardless of whether they are Jew or Gentile.

Most striking throughout Luke's Gospel is the focus on addressing the issues or problems of this world. In Luke, salvation happens in this world when the problems in society are addressed. Some of the ways this idea is communicated is with a focus on the poor and the outcast, rescuing the oppressed, much discussion about financial matters and the exploitation of the people, and perhaps through a particular interest in highlighting women, who were normally not accounted for in events that took place in public.

Women in Luke

If you are interested in some of the examples in Luke's Gospel that highlight women, the list is short but significant.

First, two women, Elizabeth and Mary, are the main characters in the first two (very long) setting-the-tone-for-all-that-follows chapters, and the announcement of Jesus' conception is given to Mary, not to Joseph.

Second, Luke has a tendency to pair stories. If there is a story about Jesus healing a man, you will see shortly thereafter a story of Jesus healing a woman. In Luke 2:22–38, we see both a male and a female prophet responding to seeing Jesus, as an infant, in the temple. In the parables about finding lost things, which are unique to Luke, men and women are the characters in the stories, not just men.

Finally, it is in Luke's Gospel that we are told that women were not only funding the travels of Jesus and his disciples but that women were disciples as well. This is huge. When you hear a story about Jesus and his disciples, you can add some women to the scene in your mind! Just because women are not mentioned in a given story does not mean that they were not there.

The first three chapters are packed with content pointing to Luke's depiction of Jesus. Much like a good introductory paragraph tells us what to expect in the body of a paper, themes important to Luke show up in this "preliminary material."

Chapter 1 has the song of praise by Mary (1:46–55) and Zechariah's prophecy in 1:68–79, both of which speak of God addressing the political injustices of this world. In chapter 2, we see the announcement to the shepherds of Jesus' birth (Luke 2:8–14). Including shepherds in this celebration is an indication of including the "least of these."

When Jesus is presented in the temple, at eight days old, both Simeon and Anna respond to the infant as the one to bring about the "consolation of Israel," which is to say, the fulfillment of the promises given to Abraham. These are "this world" promises, not spiritual salvation.

Then we have John the Baptist's announcements about who Jesus is and what he will do (3:4–6). The reference to Isaiah includes the idea of putting all people on equal footing. Throughout Luke, there is an interest in genuine repentance, which we see first with John's baptism of repentance. Notice the specific actions John endorses in order to "bear fruits worthy of repentance" (3:8): share your clothing with those in need, tax collectors are to collect only the necessary amount, and soldiers are to be satisfied with their wages.

The third chapter closes with Luke's genealogy, which makes a strong appeal to Jesus as savior of all people (see the discussions of "The Genealogies in Matthew and Luke" on pp. 138–39 and "Salvation in Luke" on p. 144). During a visit to his hometown synagogue, Jesus announces his platform, as he reads from the beginning of Isaiah 61:

> The Spirit of the Lord is upon me, because he has anointed me to bring good news to the poor. He has sent me to proclaim release to the captives and recovery of sight to the blind, to let the oppressed go free, to proclaim the year of the Lord's favor. (Luke 4:18–19)

In offering his interpretation of the passage, he tells everyone that, "Today this scripture has been fulfilled in your hearing" (v. 21). All these elements of "good news" are about everyday living, if you keep in mind that the year of the LORD's favor is about forgiving debts (Deut. 15). Everyone is initially quite pleased with his message. That the people seemingly turn on a dime, in reaction to Jesus, is because he then goes on to announce that these elements of social salvation are all going to be offered to the Gentiles as well. This salvation is offered to anyone who needs it.

If you continue to read parts of Luke's Gospel beyond the first four chapters, I would urge you to pay attention to the way finances play a role, how often "the poor" or "the lost" are mentioned, and how often bodily needs are a part of the issues that Jesus addresses. Luke 19–21 is excellent for such purposes, but keep in mind that some of the things Jesus talks about, whether in parable or in regular conversation, he is critiquing, not affirming.

The Depiction of Jews in the Newer Testament

It is important to keep in mind both why the Jews of the first century might not have liked the idea that God had changed who the covenant was for and why the Gospels have content depicting Jews in some rather negative ways. On the first issue, the Jews had been God's people for around 1,800 years at that point, according to their scriptures. When Paul claimed that it was open to all people now, I hope that you can appreciate that it might seem as if God was changing his commitment to them.

The issue of why the Jews are depicted in negative ways, at times, is a bit more complicated, and we cannot know all the motivations for it. Part of the reason Luke does this is to offer a depiction of Jesus endorsing bringing the Gentiles into the covenant, even when his own people do not understand it.

As we will see in John's Gospel, Jesus himself is depicted as calling the Jewish leaders "children of the devil," and they are depicted as stubborn, pugnacious men who were constantly trying to kill Jesus. Some of those elements in the Gospels reflect the tension that developed over time between the sects of Judaism after Jesus' death more than they do what Jesus might have actually said to his fellow Jews. I cannot overstate the importance of this distinction.

It makes me nervous every time I see Jews being depicted in negative ways in the Newer Testament. The history of the conflicts between Christians and Jews long predates the Holocaust of the mid-twentieth century and is well grounded in some of the passages in the Newer Testament. Keep in mind that Judaism existed first, and Christianity took its covenant and scriptures and, essentially, turned them against the Jews. It is worth your time to consider the dynamics of how Christianity developed out of Judaism and how Newer Testament writings reflect this growth.

For instance, the story of the "wicked tenants" (Luke 20:9–19) can be read as a critique of the way the temple leaders acquire land in far-off places and continue to exploit the labor of the people in those areas. If a family has no money to pay their annual taxes, then the land they live on goes into the treasury of the temple as payment. If the new owners, the temple leaders, want to make the land productive, they will have to hire people to work it for them. When the new owners send someone to collect the produce, the people working the land do not "pay up." But why? If they couldn't produce enough from it to live on and pay taxes

Salvation in Luke

One of my favorite topics to talk about from the Newer Testament is Luke's depiction of salvation. Luke defines salvation differently than John does. This element alone might give you reason to pause.

John's salvation happens on a spiritual level. It is all about believing the right thing in order to get into heaven when you die. Luke's definition of salvation focuses on actions in this world that address systemic violence or injustice. Addressing a social wrong gives someone salvation (from that injustice) in Luke. This understanding of salvation requires action, not just belief. This might explain part of why it is less popular.

Two sections in Luke make this definition of salvation pretty clear, though it is also scattered throughout Luke's Gospel. The first four chapters, discussed above, highlight the idea that salvation happens when the problems of this world are addressed. The other great example of it is the story of Zacchaeus.

In my first full semester in seminary, one of my final papers was on the Zacchaeus story. The element of that passage that confounded me, at the time, was what was meant by the phrase, "Today, salvation has come to this house" (Luke 19:9). It was not until my second year in seminary that I could wrap my mind around "salvation" being something other than believing that Jesus died for my sins, as John's Gospel so clearly says.

Here are a few points to keep in mind as you read this story. As a chief tax collector, Zacchaeus was not just over-taxing his fellow Jews. In doing so, he was also contributing to their continued dominance by the Romans, since collection of taxes for Rome had been placed on the shoulders of the temple leaders. When Jesus announces that he will stay with Zacchaeus, he does so as the one seeking to save "the lost."

Notice how practical Zacchaeus' resolutions are after spending the afternoon with Jesus. He resolves to give half of his possessions to the poor and pay back the people he stole from, plus interest. What is it about these claims that brings salvation to his house? Zacchaeus was going to address his harmful actions and no longer contribute to the exploitation of his people.

Since salvation came to Zacchaeus' house that day, salvation is not tied to Jesus' death in Luke. By no longer participating in or benefitting from systems that oppress other people, and doing what you can to dismantle those systems that oppress, you are bringing salvation into the world, according to Luke.

before, how in the world will there be enough to also give the landowner "his share"? Instead of seeing this parable as a spiritualized story of the Jews, the covenant, and the Christians (as is common), try reading this story as a critique of the unfair taxation system that puts people into situations of extreme poverty. There is a great deal of violence in this story, but I think Jesus is commenting on how and why this happens, in the face of such unjust situations. I find that the story makes more sense this way, and the concern for addressing the social and economic injustices of the time does translate well to our context quite nicely.

Take a similar approach to the story of Jesus' triumphal entry into Jerusalem and his "cleansing" of the temple the next morning. Jesus rode into Jerusalem on the same day that Pilate would have arrived. If the platform that Jesus announced in Luke 4 is to be trusted, then his actions ought to be seen as countering or calling to account the oppressive and exploitative actions of their own leaders and those of the Roman Empire. Jesus' entry was a march of peace, countering the entry of Pilate as representative of the Roman Empire. In the same vein, calling the temple a "den of robbers" is saying that that is where the robbers themselves live and are safe. The temple leadership was forced into collaborating with the Roman Empire, and it meant they were responsible, in part, for the weighty exploitation of the Jewish people.

The end of Luke 20 is a short denouncement of the scribes, who "devour widows' houses and for the sake of appearance say long prayers. They will receive the greater condemnation" (20:47). How is it that the scribes could "devour widows' houses"? When those women had nothing else left to pay the temple taxes, their property would go to the temple treasury. Immediately after pronouncing the way widows' property is "devoured," Jesus looks up and sees people paying their "gifts" and taxes into the temple treasury. When he comments about how a poor widow puts in more than all the rich people, I suggest he is not commending her faith (as many people read that verse). Rather, he is decrying the unfair taxation system that would require that she put in all she has to live on, which means that her house is next (Luke 21:1–4).

JOHN

John's Gospel is perhaps the most beloved by many Christians today. It is certainly full of quotable verses, especially the "I am" phrases, such as, "I am the way, the truth, and the life," and "I am the light of the world." Then there are the well-loved lines, "you will know the truth and the truth will set you free," and John 3:16, "for God so loved the world. . . ." So I will tread lightly here as I invite you to think about John from a new perspective. As with every other topic in this book, I am simply inviting you to take a fresh look at a particular part of the Bible and to consider it and its implications for yourself. The more dear a passage is to you, however, the more difficult it can be to do this.

John depicts Jesus as the Man Sent from Heaven. He is a divine being who has descended to earth, taken on human form, will fulfill the task he was sent to carry out, and then will return to the heavenly realm. Sometimes people refer to this pattern as an ascending/descending motif, which is used in many ancient myths to speak about the way gods interacted with humans. Given the above/below pattern throughout, the way Jesus talks in John takes on both a highly dualistic and a spiritualized perspective when compared to the way he speaks in the Synoptic Gospels.

Son of Man

The first order of business is to clarify the "Man" sent from heaven bit. This is addressed in chart 6, on page 135, in the Mark section as well. To summarize, "Son of God" was applied to humans, and "Son of Man" refers to a God or a divine being visiting the earth. In other words, it sounds somewhat backwards to most people. Additionally, making this distinction is somewhat irrelevant for most Christians, since they ascribe both labels to Jesus. But in terms of what we see in the four Gospels, only John is absolutely clear about calling Jesus "God," both through the way Son of Man is used and in the way Jesus identifies with God.

Word of God

Take a look at the beginning of John, as you did for Matthew and Luke. Reading John 1:1–18 as if it is a birth narrative puts Jesus in a cosmic realm from the beginning of time. This Jesus was with God "in the beginning" and everything was created by and through this Jesus, who is also called the "Word": "In the beginning was the word and the word was moving toward God and the word was God" (John 1:1, author's translation). There are many applications of "the word of God" in Christian traditions today, but none that I know of use it in the way it was being used in John initially!

In the Greek of John 1, the term used is *logos* (not capitalized in the Greek). Many English words draw on this term, *logos*. Biology is the study or the things (*logos*) pertaining to life (*bios*). In ancient thought, *logos* referred to a "thing," "word," or "matter" (tangible material), and even to "reason" or "mind" (as in, the part of your head that you think with). An ancient approach to this *logos*, as talked about in John 1, sees it as cosmic material that existed before the creation of the world. It was semi-divine and was the material used to create the universe. This *logos* was good and was drawn toward the Good.

As you can imagine, this way of talking about Jesus had an appeal to Greek-minded folks. It is worth thinking through the initial idea, especially in light of how different it is from what people, today, tend to mean when they call Jesus or passages from the Bible "the Word of God."

"I Am" Statements

For the sake of this conversation, I am not interested in sorting through all the specific "I am" statements throughout John's Gospel. I am more interested in having you think about what these statements in general tell us about John's depiction of Jesus.

John's Jesus—fully aware of who he is and claiming his identity, directly and often, throughout the Gospel—stands in rather stark contrast to the "messianic secret" version of Jesus in Mark. Take a moment to think about this. It becomes a bit difficult to reconcile this aspect of Mark's depiction of Jesus with John's as existing in the same person, but for the messages each Gospel writer was trying to convey, these conflicting descriptions make perfect sense.

Ascending/Descending Motif

Jesus' conversation with Nicodemus in John 3:1–10 is the first clear example of this motif. Their exchange starts out with Nicodemus indicating that he knows that Jesus must have come from God (above), since the signs that Jesus performed could be explained only by a connection to God. But Jesus takes the conversation in a different direction and talks about being born from above. For people who have grown up thinking about these ideas, saying that someone must be born from above or born of the Spirit makes perfect sense. But at the time that John was written, these were ideas found in Greek, and perhaps early Gnostic, thought, which were being

Eating Jesus' Flesh and Drinking His Blood?!

I love to discuss John 6:52–58, not because I am a fan of gore, but because most people are unaware that these words are attributed to Jesus. Take a few moments to read through it, once or twice.

Let's get the obvious issue out of the way: Was Jesus expecting people to start gnawing on his arm and tapping his veins for blood? No. I do not think so. But if you read through these verses a couple times, it does sound as if he means it all quite literally, doesn't it? There are three points about this passage that you might find interesting.

First, some early followers of Jesus were accused of being cannibals. Yes, cannibals. Perhaps you can understand why, given a passage such as this one.

Second, the belief in transubstantiation is based on this passage. Transubstantiation is the belief that the substance of the bread used for the Eucharist (or Communion) transforms into Jesus' body in a rather literal sense. The same goes for the wine transforming into his blood. Regardless of whether you believe such alchemy can take place every time Mass is celebrated around the world, it is good to know that the belief that it can and does happen comes from taking this passage quite literally.

Third, this idea is adapted from Greco-Roman traditions. As with so many ideas related to Jesus, I had assumed that this idea of ingesting his body and blood, in order to abide in him and he in us, was unique to Jesus. How unsettling to keep finding out that assumption was incorrect! One of the best examples is found in the initiation ceremony for followers of Mithras, which long predates Jesus. They believed that ingesting the body and blood of a slaughtered bull, which represented the strength and fertility of Mithras, made the worshiper one with the god. The god dwelt in him and he in the god.

To be clear: anytime we see beliefs or practices in Christianity that were not a part of the Jewish tradition, we can be certain that those new beliefs came from Greco-Roman religions. This is one of those beliefs. A belief does not have to be unique to your faith system in order for it to be meaningful.

For further reading about similarities between Christian beliefs and elements of Greco-Roman religions, I recommend Anna Tripolitis's *Religions of the Hellenistic-Roman Age* (Eerdmans, 2001).

adapted to belief about Jesus. This was not an idea found in the scriptures that Jesus knew and would have struck most Jews as rather odd.

Note Jesus' response to Nicodemus in John 3:13: "No one has ascended into heaven except the one who descended from heaven, the Son of Man." The remainder of chapter 3 is worth reading, to look for both this ascending/descending motif and the dualistic content, discussed below.

Think about what this motif says about Jesus and how different it is from the Synoptics' depiction of him. Some additional examples include: 1:51; 3:11–13, 31–36; 5:22–37; 6:29–63; 7:28–33; 8:23–24; 9:4–5; 10:44–50; 13:3; 17:1–5. Also keep in mind that it is the latest of the canonical Gospels to be written, thus it would make sense for it to reflect the most development of thought or belief associated with Jesus.

Dualistic Worldview

Dualism, as it applies to a person's worldview, is the belief or idea that everything has two opposite parts, or that everything can be talked about as "fitting into" one of two opposites, with no place for in-betweens. For instance, there is a good deal of talk about light and darkness or spirit versus flesh in John, as well as the above/below motif. I invite you to take a few minutes to fill in a few more dualisms in chart 7 from everyday life that you can think of.

Chart 7: Sets of Dualisms

Light	Dark
Heaven/Above	Earth/Below
Spirit	Flesh
Right	Wrong

Perhaps your pairs included man/woman, God/humans, hot/cold, white/black, heterosexual/LGBTQ, and so forth. Did you pay attention to which word you put in the left column? Western cultures tend to think of one column as representing what is "good," and the other is deemed "bad" or negative.

This kind of dualistic worldview is quite different from the yin-yang worldview common in Eastern cultures. The main difference is that in the yin-yang concept, both sides are valued as necessary. Thus neither is judged to be good or bad.

There are three things about this dualistic worldview that I invite you to contemplate. First, as I just indicated, notice the value or judgment sometimes ascribed to elements of a dualism. Is the man/woman dualism appropriately given a good/bad valuation? What about white/black? Does the culture you are a part of value the spiritual realm more than flesh and bones?

Second, strict dualisms do not accurately describe reality. For children, up to about the age of ten, the world needs to be talked about in these overly simplistic ways. They cannot fully handle the nuances that an adult mind regularly sorts through. But aren't there plenty of shades of light and dark in this world? We do not go from daylight to pitch dark, for instance. Something similar can be said for any of the sets of dualisms. Our world is much more complex than dualisms allow for.

Third, consider how the first two, unchallenged and taken together, can influence how a person sees the world and interacts with others. For instance, what if, in your world, men actually were considered better or more valued than women? How would that influence the way you think about women's abilities or contributions in comparison to men's? What if the light really were better than the dark? Would you ever seek the dark stillness of a night in an open field, gazing at stars? If you see all beliefs as either "right" or "wrong," how might you interact with people with beliefs different than your own?

This all or nothing—you're either with us or against us—thinking will end up playing out in other parts of a person's life, beyond one's beliefs. Dualistic thinking is appropriate for children; it is insufficient for mature adults, and thus I suggest it is not appropriate to maintain in a mature faith system.

Look at some of the dualistic references in the Gospel of John and think through possible effects they could have on people who take them seriously and quite literally as faithful disciples of Jesus Christ: John 1:1–13; 3:5–7, 19–21, 31–36; 6:63; 8:21–47; 14:23–24; 15:5–6, 18–19; 17:14–16.

Chart 8: Comparing the "Essences of Jesus"

	Mark	Matthew	Luke	John
Essence	Misunderstood, Suffering Son of God	Jewish Messiah	Savior of the World	Man Sent from Heaven
Ways This Essence Is Depicted	"Messianic Secret"	Lineage begins with Abraham Parallel to Moses' life Fulfillment citations Fulfilling righteousness Affirming the Law	Lineage goes all the way back to God/ includes all people Clearly depicted as being sent to the nations, not just the Jews Seeking and saving "the lost"	Descending/ascending motif Numerous "I am" sayings Jesus is clearly equal to God Jesus talks about completing the job he was sent into the world to accomplish
Other Notable Characteristics of the Gospel			Salvation is found in addressing injustices	Judgment or salvation depends on belief Dualisms

Conclusion to John

The main things about John's Gospel that I have endeavored to high-light are how starkly different this depiction of Jesus is from the Syn-optic Gospel depictions and the underlying dualistic "you're with us or against us" worldview of John. Given how popular John's Gospel is for so many Christians, it is worth your time to think through these elements of John.

CONCLUSION

When you consider that all these ways of understanding Jesus are in the Bible, it makes it difficult to know who is meant by the claim that someone "believes in Jesus." Usually, the Jesus that person is refer-ring to will be the one found in John: the one who was God incarnate who just asks you to believe the right things about him and to accept him as your savior. But this is not the only depiction of Jesus in the Newer Testament. There is a strong tradition and depiction of Jesus as a person calling for social reform; and financial matters figure fairly prominently in these depictions of what Jesus cares about. I think it is worth your while to spend some time thinking about the fact that the "believe in me" Jesus is the latest of the four to enter the picture and is a far cry from the first depiction that we find in Mark, for instance.

I hope this more complex, and hopefully richer, view of Jesus and the Gospels will give you plenty of food for thought and fuel for your faith.

 TAKE THE BIBLE INTO YOUR OWN HANDS

1. Does the ancient approach to biography, with a specific angle on the person in mind, make such stories less true or compelling for you? How does this approach to ancient biographies impact the way you might read the Gospels in the future?

2. Does the fact that the Gospel writers used multiple sources, both written and verbal, change the way you view scripture as "inspired"?

Does one Gospel's portrayal of Jesus appeal to you more than the others? Why is that?

3. What significance do you see in the Gospel writers' use of Jewish, Greek, and Roman stories and images? Do you think Matthew's connection between Moses and Jesus is coincidental or intentional?

4. How do the terms we use to describe Jesus—Son of God, Son of Man, Messiah, Savior, Word—shape the way we think of Jesus today? Does it matter if our understandings of these terms differ from their original intent?

5. What is your understanding of salvation? Which Gospel has most shaped your beliefs on the subject?

6. How do you think we should handle the dualistic content in John's Gospel?

10

Was Paul the First Christian?

The time has come to talk about Paul. Paul: the Apostle to the Gentiles; the man who had a dramatic conversion moment on the road to Damascus. Paul who was previously Saul. Paul to whom thirteen of the twenty-seven Newer Testament writings are attributed. (Several early Church Fathers thought that he also wrote Hebrews, though this view is not widely endorsed today.) Paul is a man that many people, based on a few selections from Newer Testament letters that we have already discussed, assume was anti-women. Others credit him with endorsing equality between men and women in leadership within the churches. He is called the creator of Christianity by some people, the first Christian by others, and not a Christian at all by still others. Paul has gotten a great deal of attention over the years, with good reason.

We can't discuss in this one chapter every juicy issue related to Paul. The pressing matter of women in leadership in the Church I address in chapter 7; some of his ideas about sex and sexuality are included in chapter 4. For this chapter, the three points of discussion are the matters related to what people call his "conversion moment," the dynamic between Paul and Jesus' disciples, and what "Paul's gospel" was all about. If at any point a suggestion that I make challenges what you have always thought about Paul, I hope you will go for the "educated mind" response and at least entertain the idea.

PAUL'S "CONVERSION MOMENT"

Take a few moments to sort through what you have been told or what you believe to be the story related to Paul and his "conversion moment." Are there details in his story that have stuck with you, in terms of being essential parts of it? Do you know who is telling the story? What exactly did he convert from and to in this moment?

One of the most fascinating parts about Paul and this conversion moment, it seems to me, is the source of this story. You see, the dramatic flash-of-light and voice-from-the-heavens version comes in the book of Acts, which was written down about fifty years after the event, and not by Paul himself. Actually, there are three slightly different versions of this moment in Acts (9:1–30; 22:1–21; 26:12–23). I hope you will read through these accounts for yourself. The small changes in details can be explained, instead of fretted over, by keeping in mind that someone other than Paul wrote Acts and that what matters most is the general outcome of the event, not the details. But, for those who want to hold on to a belief that the Bible is "free from errors or contradictions," these differences would prove a bit tricky to explain away.

In Paul's own writings, we get no sense of something miraculous happening to him or around him. He merely speaks of how at one point he was persecuting the followers of Jesus, and then, in response to God revealing the Son in him, he decided to take a message about Christ to the Gentiles instead. The main content from Paul's letters that addresses his "conversion" moment is found in Galatians 1:13–20. I encourage you to read it thoughtfully, with an eye toward which source is more reliable, Paul or Acts.

There are three elements of the Galatians passage that are of distinct importance for this conversation. The first is how to interpret the line, "my earlier life in Judaism." Though simple, it can be read in two distinctly different ways. One suggests that Judaism was a part of his earlier life but is no longer relevant to him. The other says that he still sees himself as living in Judaism, and he is merely referring to an earlier time in his life. His reference to the church of God (not of Christ) is another indication that even for Paul, the "church" is a part of Judaism.

The second point about the Galatians passage is when Paul says that God revealed his Son "in" him. Perhaps this does not differ from something being revealed "to" someone. But take a moment to think this through. Which seems more plausible: the version Paul hints at, which is an internal revelation, akin to an epiphany; or a voice booming down to him from the heavens, as Acts suggests? Of course, many people today will refer to the way God speaks to them, usually through prayer or as moments of insight that come to them out of the blue. But do any of these people literally hear a voice out loud? Wouldn't we wonder about their mental stability if they claimed to? I'm inclined to go with Paul's version, not Acts', on this bit. What about you?

The third issue is the order of events. Paul says that God revealed his Son in him and that he went into Arabia, then on to Damascus. He says that it was another three years before he went to Jerusalem. While he was there, he stayed with Cephas (Peter) and met only one other disciple: James, Jesus' brother. He seems rather insistent about his version of events. But they do not line up, in important places, with what Acts says.

Acts tells us that Paul saw a bright light and heard a voice and fell to the ground. After being helped up, he went directly into Damascus, and from there he went to Jerusalem. According to Acts 9:26–30, Barnabus introduced Paul to all of Jesus' disciples in Jerusalem, and Paul told them about how he saw and heard from Jesus. Paul freely "went in and out among them in Jerusalem" (v. 28).

Beyond the Arabia visit, what do you make of the differences in these accounts of Paul's life? Paul claims that he knew only Peter and James. Acts suggests that he knew them all quite well. Paul insists that his message is his own, but the stories in Acts indicate that he consulted with the disciples and apostles early on and regularly. Though subtle, those are important distinctions to make.

With these points noted, let me remind you that the question at hand is whether or not we should think of Paul as having had a "conversion moment." To that end, some of the things that Paul says in other letters are helpful to include here. In 2 Corinthians 11:21–23, he discusses how he can trump anyone who has something to boast about as an apostle, but in doing so, he affirms his identity as a Hebrew, an Israelite, and a descendant of Abraham, first and foremost.

There is also the Romans 9:1–5 passage, where Paul discusses his "own people," the Israelites/Jews. When we take into consideration that Judaism is a tradition and identity you are born into (notwithstanding that people today choose to convert into it), it does make it difficult to suggest that Paul saw himself giving up this part of his identity. His mission to be a messenger or minister of Christ simply means that he brought a message of Christ to those who needed it. By Paul's own claims regarding how a person is made a part of the covenant with God, Jews did not need Christ; Gentiles did.

Thus, by Paul's own definition, he not only was not, but could not be, a "Christian." Being such would be to misunderstand the whole point of the Torah, which was the gift to the Jews, and the death of Christ, which was the gift to the Gentiles as their way into the covenant. What Paul was talking to Gentiles about was not a separate religion. He was talking to Gentiles about joining the promises of Judaism. Thus, his message led to a new sect of Judaism! In the early second century, after several decades of what we could call sectarian fighting, the sect of Judaism that worshiped Jesus and the sects that did not finally parted ways. It is not until this parting, however, that we can strictly speak of "Christianity." Up until then, "Christianity" was still a sect of Judaism.

Throw into the mix the issue that the term *Christian* was originally used by a Jew, or a group of Jews, in 67 CE to refer to those Jews-who-worship-Jesus, specifically in the congregation that met in Syrian Antioch. It was initially a slur or an epithet. Like so many slurs, this one was brazenly claimed and championed by those it referred to. But whether Paul was still alive, or if he died in the Neroian persecution in Rome (64–68 CE) as we suspect, it is worth considering the original context and meaning of the label.

It seems to me that the moment Paul changed his course has been erroneously referred to as a "conversion" for Paul. Yes, there was a change of heart and a change of mission. But it's not the same thing as converting from one form of religious identity to another, as most people think of conversions today. If you would like to look into this matter further, I suggest you read Pamela Eisenbaum's *Paul Was Not a Christian*.

PAUL AND JESUS' DISCIPLES

On this topic, I need to begin by asking you to think about how two thousand years of tradition might influence what people are willing to see or consider. I find it productive to consciously start with what we find in the Bible before jumping into the conclusions that have been passed along based on them. What the Bible tells us about the dynamic between Paul and Jesus' own disciples might surprise you. I'll begin with what is in Paul's writings on this matter.

In Galatians 1:18–19, Paul claims that he initially had contact with Peter and James but none of the others. Keep in mind how much Paul insists, time after time in his letters, that he did not confer with anyone else in terms of receiving both his "marching orders" to go to the Gentiles and the content of the message that he proclaimed. This is an important point. Paul was quite confident that his message was correct (which implies that there is at least one message out there that he thought was wrong), and one of the ways he asserted this was to remind people that he didn't interact much with Jesus' own disciples. Hmmm.

There is one distinct issue that shows up in most of Paul's letters: circumcision. "The circumcised" is a way to refer to the Jews. The question of whether or not the Gentiles need to be circumcised comes up in Galatians 2:1–9; 5:2–12; Romans 2–4; 1 Corinthians 7:18–19; and Philippians 3:1–5. Even at the end of the first century, in the disputed Pauline letters, we see this issue continue. Ephesians 2:11 specifically labels Jews and Gentiles as "the circumcision" and "the uncircumcision," respectively. Titus 1:10–11 says that people who endorse circumcision are "rebellious people," teaching things that are not right to teach.

Many people today are not clear as to why circumcision was such a big deal, so here's the scoop. It is a defining characteristic or outward sign of Abraham's (and thus all his male descendants') commitment to the covenant with Yahweh. Genesis 17:1–14 makes it clear that in order to be a part of this covenant, males must be circumcised. Likewise, any male not circumcised has broken the covenant with God and shall be cut off from the people. Circumcision was as essential to Judaism as "being saved" is to an Evangelical today.

So when Paul says that Gentiles can be brought into God's covenant with the descendants of Israel, you can see why some devout Jews at the time, which included Jesus' own disciples, would have assumed that the newcomers would submit themselves to circumcision.

To highlight that Paul and Jesus' disciples saw this issue somewhat differently, look at what Paul says in Galatians 2. He talks about going to Jerusalem a second time, in order to discuss with the "acknowledged leaders" the message he was proclaiming to the Gentiles. (Acts 15 confirms that this is quite an important meeting of the minds.) Paul wanted to be sure the Jerusalem faction approved of his message. He notes that "even Titus . . . was not compelled to be circumcised, though he was a Greek" (Gal. 2:3). Paul also asserts that some "false believers" were slipped into the deliberations. Spies and summits and shaking hands of agreement. These are serious matters, and Paul asserts again that he took no insights or direction from those acknowledged leaders: Peter, James, and John.

To further the point, Paul explains how he and Peter butted heads when Peter visited the congregation in Syrian Antioch—Paul's home congregation (Gal. 2:11–14). When Peter, a Jew, first arrived in Antioch, he ate with Gentiles. But when some friends from Jerusalem came to check up on him, he stopped. If Jews were not certain that they could eat with "the uncircumcised," this meant that they were not entirely sold on there being unity between them. Apparently, Paul chewed out Peter over this issue, calling him a hypocrite.

The bottom line is that during Paul's lifetime, the details had not been hammered out. There was still a great deal of tension and confusion regarding what it looked like to have Jews and Gentiles joined together under one promise or covenant. The way Paul tells the story, Peter and Paul had fundamentally different convictions on the circumcision issue.

Fun Fact

The space where the church in Antioch initially met is still in use today. This is the church that Paul used as his home base, and it is members of this congregation who were originally labeled "Christians." The space itself is a cave in the side of a mountain.

Interestingly enough, that church is now called St. Peter's. Given the clash between these two, I do wonder if this has Paul constantly spinning in his grave. What do you think?

The circumcision-faction dynamic was an issue in places beyond the region of Galatia. In 2 Corinthians 10–13, Paul refers to some people he calls "super-apostles." These four chapters express Paul's frustration with the people in Corinth for listening to, and believing in, a message other than Paul's. Paul reacts, and quite passionately, to other apostles having come along behind Paul in his travels and telling the Gentiles that if they want to join in the party—that is, to be a part of this covenant with God—then they must also circumcise themselves. Hmmm. This makes Paul furious for two reasons. The first reason is that people are not trusting him and everything he said to them. The second reason is that in trusting these other "super-apostles" who came along after him, these Gentiles-now-a-part-of-the-covenant have misunderstood the whole system that Paul has presented.

To be clear, we do not know with any certainty who the label "super-apostles" refers to. What we can be certain of, however, is that as Paul traveled around the Mediterranean world, there were followers of Jesus who did not fully agree with Paul's message to the Gentiles and that the primary issue was whether or not Gentiles should also be circumcised as a sign of their commitment to the covenant. Fighting over this element, circumcision, was a way for Jews to express resistance to what Paul was saying and doing. From their perspective, the nature of the whole system related to being a part of the covenant was being challenged or changed by Paul's message to the Gentiles. Paul and Jesus' own disciples did not see this inclusion of the Gentiles in the same way.

There is one final fascinating tidbit in this conversation that I would like you to consider. Paul's genuine letters were all written before Mark, the earliest Gospel, was written down. What this means is that while stories about Jesus had been passed along for years, they were not committed to writing until after Romans, 1 and 2 Corinthians, Galatians, Philippians, 1 Thessalonians, and Philemon had been written. Interpreting Jesus' execution and resurrection is something that Paul did, for the Gentiles, in person, and sometimes again in those letters. The narratives of the Gospels bring Jesus' life and his disciples into the picture to flesh it out a bit and connect the whole story to Jesus' people, the Jews.

If we want to see how Jesus' own disciples viewed Paul, we are somewhat out of luck! We do not know, with any certainty, of anything in the Newer Testament being written by one of the men who traveled around with Jesus. The Gospels of Matthew and John are simply attributed to those names; we do not know who actually wrote them. The same goes for the letters of 1 and 2 Peter and James. Regardless, Paul is not mentioned in the Gospels or in letters not attributed to him. The closest we can come is to looking at what is recorded in Acts, and I have already suggested that you take its depiction of Paul with a grain of salt.

Regardless of whether Paul and Jesus' own disciples got along or had the same vision for the Gentiles, the possibility that they did not and Paul's confidence in the correctness of his own message provide much fodder for contemplation.

PAUL'S "GOSPEL"

What does it mean that Paul was sent as the apostle to the Gentiles? What, exactly, was the content of his message that would have been "good news" for them? Did it sound the same to them as it does to us today?

First, let's discuss this term *gospel*, which comes from the Greek word *euangelion*. Yes, it means "good news." But in what way is it good news? In the ancient world, this term would apply to anything in the political or social landscape—including news of victory in battle or even the birth of a son for the emperor. Many Christians today might respond with something along the lines of, "It is good news of salvation!" Salvation is also a term that can be, and is, understood in many ways today. Salvation for an Evangelical, for instance, usually focuses on the soul "being saved" (from eternal damnation and torment) after the person dies. Salvation for other Christians today means addressing the systems of injustice here on earth. While you might disagree with one of these views, it is noteworthy that there is such a range of interpretation of this term that comes from scripture, isn't it?

Paul's message, of "good news" for the Gentiles, was different in content from the good news for Jews. We know that this is the case because of the way Jews and Gentiles are brought into the covenant. They had different ways, or means, of being granted admission. This perspective is seen as Paul discusses the role of circumcision in Galatians 5:2–12, for instance. It is pretty clear that the Law/Torah (and thus circumcision) applies only to Jews, and grace or salvation through Christ is for Gentiles. Any Gentile who tried to uphold the Law, and thus sought to be circumcised, was simply missing the point. "Listen! I, Paul, am telling you that if you let yourselves be circumcised, Christ will be of no benefit to you. . . . You who want to be justified by the law have cut yourselves off from Christ; you have fallen away from grace" (Gal. 5:2, 4). It seems to me that Paul often speaks in rather dramatic terms in order to make his point, as he does here: Gentiles seeking to keep the law have "fallen from grace" or are obedient to the wrong thing.

Whatever you wish to do with this Jew/Gentile bit, it is the matter of salvation in Christ that I would like you to think about for a moment. What, exactly, is happening in this idea? Or, as some students have asked: to what and from what are people being saved? This may be something you have spent a great deal of time thinking about; it might be something you have simply heard and accepted. Whatever the case, I invite you to think through how Paul discusses Jesus' death and resurrection as a means of salvation.

Chart 9 helps you see how Paul discusses "salvation" or the redeemed life. You might be surprised to see that he uses several distinct models or ways of discussing how Jesus' death, blood, and resurrection bring about salvation for others. Only one of these is grounded in the Jewish scriptures. All the rest Paul seems to have borrowed from Greek and Roman religious traditions.

Chart 9: Models of Salvation

Model	How Sin Is Discussed	How Jesus "Solves" the Problem of Sin	Our Role	Scripture
Judicial	Human disobedience (sinfulness) requires death as a punishment	Jesus' death is on our behalf; the penalty or punishment of death that our sinfulness deserves, he takes on himself	Accept it as a gift	Romans 3:23; 5:18–21
Participationist	Sin is a cosmic power that has influence over us	Jesus' death and resurrection shows God's power is victorious over sin and death	Through baptism we "participate" in Jesus' death and resurrection, thus taking power over sin as well	Romans 6:3–14
Reconciliation (Justification)	Humans and God had a falling out; God is mad at us for our sin	In dying, Jesus makes it possible for humans and God to be in relationship again	Accept and believe that this is true	Romans 5:10–21; 8:32–33
Redemption	We are enslaved to sin/the devil, we belong to it/him	Jesus' blood is the price to buy us, purchase us, from it/him	Believe that this has been done	Romans 3:9–24; 6:15–23 Romans 7
Atonement / Sacrifice	Sin is just something we have done, which has severed our relationship with God	Jesus' blood covers over the people and brings us back together with God: at-one-ment	Accept/believe that Jesus' spilt blood appeases God's anger at our sin	Romans 3:24–25a; 1 Corinthians 10:16

As you look through these models of salvation, I hope you will think through what each one assumes about humanity and God and what it takes for humans and God to relate to one another. For instance, in the judicial model, do you know where the idea comes from that says that human disobedience ought to be repaid with death (whether physical or spiritual)? Stop and think about this for a moment. Certainly this topic touches on issues of "free will" and "human nature" and even grace. But why would someone suggest to you that part of who we are as humans deserves that kind of a punishment? This model plays out in such a way that Jesus took on himself our "just" punishment, and to receive the benefit of such a gift, we must accept the gift appropriately. Thus, anyone who is not duly grateful for his obedience and sacrifice is offending God once again. It's a fascinating problem/solution set, wouldn't you say?

Also fascinating is the final model, Atonement/Sacrifice, which we discussed in chapter 5, and I think that it bears repeating. It seems to me that we ought to look closely at, and perhaps reconsider, talking about sacrificing a life as a means to bringing God and humanity back into relations with each other. The mere suggestion that one life must be taken—whether it is an animal or Jesus, as the Lamb of God—in order for reconciliation to happen is somewhat counter-intuitive. Taking a life in order to promote life? In fact, this idea of needing Jesus' death as an essential component of forgiveness means that Christianity is a *thanophilic* religion. The term *thanophilic* means "loving death." This might seem a bit extreme, especially the first time you hear it. But it is an accurate label of this view of forgiveness. Something to think about.

Aside from how we might make sense of these models of salvation, on their own or mixed together, as is typical, I hope you will think about the fact that only the final model is familiar to the Jewish tradition. What this means is that Paul incorporates concepts of salvation that were already familiar to the Gentiles he was trying to reach. It is a smart move to make. It is also using ideas that were foreign to Jesus' own tradition to make sense of Jesus' death. Hmmm. From the perspective of other Jews at the time, can you see why this would seem a bit unsettling?

I do not think we need to be thrown by the fact that much of the way Paul made sense of Jesus' death and resurrection came from Greek or Roman religious ideas. This form of appropriating the ideas of other cultures has continually happened throughout the existence of humankind. What I do find to be productive, and hopefully somewhat eye-opening, is a thoughtful reflection on what these models of salvation say about who God is and how Paul (and others) perceived that we relate to God. Just because they thought that in our humanness, which includes our imperfections, we have offended God beyond our own ability to make amends does not mean that they were spot on; nor does it mean that we must agree with them.

CONCLUSION

It is my hope that as a result of this chapter you will have thought about and read some of the biblical passages that talk about Paul and his change of perspective. I hope that you can at least see how some people do not think he had what we would call a conversion experience; rather he had an epiphany that led to the creation of a new sect of Judaism.

I also hope that you now see the beginnings of the Jesus movement, and what ultimately became "Christianity," in a new light. Thinking about Paul and his relationship to Jesus' own disciples is just one of many ways to get into that conversation. I hope it has proved productive for you.

It also seems to me that thinking about not just what "salvation" is but how the Church talks about it, how the doctrine of the Church affirms that it has been made possible, is a fairly important task. Words have power. The metaphors people use to talk about the relationship between God and humanity do take shape in their lives. They do inform an understanding of who human beings are and what humans are capable of being. I hope you will give yourself the gift of thinking through these things. Permission granted.

TAKE THE BIBLE INTO YOUR OWN HANDS

1. What is your understanding of Paul's role in the development of the Christian movement? Do you see Paul as a lifelong Jew or something different?

2. How do you imagine the environment and issues of the early Church? Where would you see yourself in the Jew-Gentile dynamic? How is the debate over circumcision different from and similar to debates we have among factions of the Church today?

3. Why does it matter if Paul and Jesus' own disciples agreed on the message of the Gospel for the Gentiles? How do you describe the difference between Paul's "gospel" and the message of Jesus expressed by his own followers? Does the fact that Paul's letters were written before the Gospels have significance to you?

4. How do you define *human sin* and *salvation*? Is it similar to one or more of the models described in the above chart? What do these different models of how Paul talked about salvation assume about humans and our ability to relate to God? Do you agree with him?

11

Judgment Day Is . . . Not Coming

It just so happens that I began this chapter immediately after completing season 6 of *Dexter* (thank you, Showtime, via Netflix). For those of you not familiar with the show, it is one of the most appallingly appealing shows I have ever been addicted to. The main premise is that a forensic blood-spatter analyst, who happens to work for the Miami Metro Police force, is also a serial killer . . . mostly of serial killers. Right. So, while I am not trying to endorse vigilante justice, which is one of many complex issues this show takes on, you can perhaps see why so many people are hooked on the show once they watch an episode or two.

I tell you all this because the murderer who is the main focus of season 6 is a religious fanatic who depicts scenes from the book of Revelation using dead bodies. To be fair, this person is also depicted as a sociopath who has had psychic breaks with reality and is off of his medication. Regardless, there is still a reason the writers of this award-winning series chose this topic to play with and could do so for twelve episodes.

You do not have to look very far to find the idea of "an Apocalypse" being depicted in our culture. Depending on your taste, you can turn to the somewhat-true-to-Revelation form as depicted by *Dexter*, captured in the *Left Behind* series, and found in various movies over the years, such as *End of Days*, *The Rapture*, and *The Seventh Sign*. There are literally hundreds of movies that apply the concept of the end of the world to our modern global crises of nuclear war, viral outbreaks, natural disasters, and climate change. Clearly this idea of humanity or the entire planet coming to an end is something fascinating to our collective consciousness.

Add to this proliferation of media various examples of collective cultural concerns about biblical "predictions" coming true. For instance, remember that paranoia leading up to "Y2K"? What about debit cards? I distinctly recall being semi-terrified during college when they were introduced. This development was interpreted by some in my faith community as a step in the direction of chips being implanted in our hands or foreheads, which was being called "the mark of the beast." You may laugh, but I recall, those first couple years, hesitating every time I used my debit card at a grocery store.

There have been countless times over the centuries when charismatic leaders found ways to apply the apocalyptic writings to their time and situation and concluded that the world would be ending on a specific day. I know of people who discussed these matters with their children, warning them and hoping their children would be "right with the Lord," since three days out would be Judgment Day. Extremist groups have gone down in blazes or mass suicides from literally "drinking the Kool-Aid" because of this way of seeing the world. It is not new to this generation, but it does not need to continue either.

As you might have guessed, "what the Bible says" on this topic and what most people think it says are actually startlingly different. I have known many people who were scared to even venture reading Revelation because of how traumatized they were by the way it was taught to them as children. While some of the scenes are a bit trippy, I certainly do not think that people should be terrified by the basic message the book of Revelation contains.

In this chapter, I will discuss some of the literary concepts of an apocalypse, and what their purpose is, before addressing some of the specific symbols from the books of Revelation and Daniel. Regardless of your perspective on this topic, you might be surprised at what you discover.

APOCALYPTIC LITERATURE

Before launching into this discussion, take some time to think through what thoughts you bring to this conversation. Perhaps see if you can answer these questions: What is the purpose of an apocalypse? Who was meant to understand the message when it was written? Why was the book of Revelation written? For whom is it relevant today?

What Is an Apocalypse?

Let's begin with defining some terms and setting some of the framework for apocalyptic stories. The word *apocalypse* comes from the Greek

---

Calling Them Christians

You may have noticed that I have in this book, for the most part, avoided using the term *Christian* when talking about Jesus' early followers. This is why:

First, Jesus himself was a Jew, and his initial disciples (the 12+ men and however many women) were also Jews. We should expect nothing other than this. The apostle Paul was also a Jew. The movement that began after Jesus' execution and resurrection, which focused on worshiping Jesus, was initially a sect of Judaism.

We see the first reference to *Christian* as a label for the followers of Jesus around the year 67 CE. As I noted in chapter 10, it was initially something of a slur used by one Jew (or group of Jews) to refer to the sect of Judaism that was focused on Jesus as the Messiah. So the question is, how quickly did any of the followers of Jesus take up the derogatory label and "own it" in order to take the negative power out of it? We have no way of knowing the answer to this question, unfortunately.

What we do know is that by around 125 CE, there was something of a mutual disowning that took place. The Jews who did not worship Jesus saw too much difference between themselves and the worshipers of Jesus. The former could no longer view the latter as *Jews*. It is not too much of a stretch to suggest that the feelings were mutual (given what we see in the writings of the Newer Testament and the early Church Fathers).

Thus, *Christianity* as something distinct from Judaism was not in existence at the time of Jesus' death or for most of the first hundred years after that. No, it takes some time for that distinction to solidify. Since most of the writings of the Newer Testament come about prior to this mutual disowning in 125 CE, and the writers themselves still seem to identify with Judaism, it makes sense to avoid using the term *Christian* when discussing them.

word *apocalypsis*, which means a "revealing" or an "unveiling." This is why the final book of the Newer Testament is called Revelation: something is revealed in the dream that John has. The metaphorical curtain separating the physical and spiritual worlds is pulled back, revealing a scene fraught with symbolic meaning. Just as they do today or in other parts of the Bible, these dreams require some interpretation.

An apocalypse is a story. It is not a literal prediction of the future. There is no reason to expect the things depicted in Revelation to actually "play out"—ever. The main purpose of apocalyptic stories in the Bible was to give the reader some hope that things are about to change. Apocalypses were written for people suffering terribly, sending them the message that God sees their suffering and is going to bring it to an end very soon.

Characteristics of Apocalyptic Literature

We also talk about this as a type of writing. So you can add "apocalyptic literature" to the list of genres we find in the Bible, specifically in Revelation and in parts of Daniel. Since it is a specific genre, we can also talk about some of the characteristics of apocalyptic writings. For instance, they are usually pseudonymous, which is to say that we usually do not know who wrote them. They were simply attributed to important and well-known people. For instance, there are apocalypses that are not in the Bible that are attributed to Moses, Abraham, and even Peter. The book of Revelation is an exception, since it opens with a reference to John (though which John is still a matter of debate).

Another characteristic of apocalypses is their inclusion of symbolic visions. What this means is that we should expect that things such as numbers, statues, and beasts are not meant to be taken literally but are representative of things in the world of the people at that time. For instance, in Revelation 1, John sees seven stars and seven lampstands, which is interpreted for the reader: the stars represent the angels who watch over the churches; the lampstands represent the churches in Asia in the first century (current western Turkey). We know that some coins from that time period depicted the emperor holding seven stars in his right hand. Since these coins pre-date the writing of Revelation, we can safely assume that John adapted the image to show Jesus as a counter to the emperor.

People often expect apocalypses to predict the way things will play out in reality, at some point. The thing is, apocalypses were not intended to be literal chronological narratives; neither were they describing things that can happen in reality. All that mattered was communicating a message that addressed the real life situation of the people.

The two most important characteristics of apocalyptic literature are the kind of life situations it is intended to address and the basic message that it sends.

First, apocalyptic literature was written for the underdogs, whose oppression was so great, and happening at the hand of such an overwhelming entity, that it seemed that the only way their situation could be addressed was if God himself entered the scene and destroyed their enemies. In the biblical examples, this suffering was at the hand of their own political leaders. I cannot overstate the importance of the political backdrop in understanding the context of apocalyptic writing. Whether the suffering they experienced was extreme financial oppression (over-taxation, unbearable interest rates) or persecution and executions, these people were trying to handle social, political, and economic realities that were too much to bear any longer.

You must admit that it sounds as if these people saw themselves as entirely powerless and hopeless. It is also important to note that, in light of some of the Inquisition-type scenarios that took place at the time of the writing of Daniel and Revelation, their fear for their lives and sense of powerlessness was somewhat reasonable.

Second, the main message of apocalypses was one of hope and encouragement. Specifically, the story was telling these people that God will, at some point in the very near future, intervene on their behalf and destroy their enemies. Immediately thereafter, God will start a new existence on earth, with these faithful few populating the new landscape. Apocalyptic literature is triumphalist. It is celebrating the idea that God will be victorious in battle. But primarily it is meant to be a message of hope that will motivate people to endure their current sufferings.

This second point is especially fascinating to me, given that so many people today read Revelation as a tool to scare people into believing in Jesus. If this application of Revelation weren't so harmful and traumatic for people, it would be humorous how much this interpretation diverges from the book's initial purposes. But I do not find it a funny matter at all. The implications of (mis)reading Revelation in this way are not only misguided but dangerous as well.

Implications of the Message of Apocalypse

I am focusing here on Revelation, since it is much more commonly drawn on than Daniel. But some of the same points can be raised in light of any apocalyptic writings. There are two sides to this hopeful and encouraging intent of apocalyptic literature that I hope you will consider.

First, how intensely extreme would your situation have to be for you to think that the only way your problems could be addressed was by God literally wiping out your enemies? You could look at this question from the angle of trying to think of what groups of people today can honestly identify with this kind of extremity. You might think of groups of people such as the Sudanese or, at the time of the writing of this book, the people in Syria. More to the point: most of today's Christians who look for Revelation to play out are not actually experiencing anything close to the same life situation that Revelation was addressing.

Second, how is it that this kind of a message can be hopeful or encouraging? My sense is that it is due to the idea that God is on one's side, God is ultimately victorious, and the people's suffering will come to an end quite soon. But I have to wonder if there isn't a more peaceful way of communicating this message, one that does not include violence, revenge, death, and destruction.

We say, today, that apocalyptic material was hopeful and encouraging for the original audiences. Why else would they be passed along in the first place? But I am not convinced that everyone saw it this way, even among the original recipients. Saying that everyone embraced apocalyptic material as encouraging is saying that everyone at the time liked violence and revenge and found some peace of mind in their "enemies" being destroyed. I am not trying to challenge that some people may have felt this way about the situation, just that perhaps not everyone was on this page.

When people want to say that apocalyptic material is useful today, they tend to overlook the initial context entirely. In addition, they are embracing a triumphalist worldview and endorsing this idea that God will be the one to destroy their enemies. Let me be clear: we are talking about a fairly extremist attitude toward resolving one's problems. When I say *extremist*, there are probably certain images that pop into your mind as a result, images of fringe groups today that deal out fear and destruction, and that connection is quite apt.

It concerns me to see people claiming that the book of Revelation comes from a God of love and accepting the content of it as something that we should expect to play out at some point.

BIBLICAL APOCALYPSES IN CONTEXT

Let's briefly consider the political situations of the original recipients of Daniel and Revelation, though most of the attention here will be directed toward Revelation. Then we will turn to discussing some of the specific symbols.

The Book of Daniel

The book of Daniel is a tricky one. It is set in the time of the Babylonian exile (approximately the seventh century BCE) but wasn't written until the mid-second century BCE, during the Jews' persecution at the hands of the Greeks.

Up until this point, the Jewish people had been conquered or carried into exile because they were on fertile land or in the middle of an important trade route. In fact, the prophets of Israel told the people, over and over again, that the reason they kept being conquered by other peoples was because they were not being faithful to Yahweh in the ways they were supposed to. The message was: if you are faithful, God has your back; and if you are experiencing suffering and oppression, it is because you are not being faithful.

During the persecution by the Greeks, however, the situation was different. It was because the people were faithful to Yahweh, their God, that they were being persecuted and executed. We see the story of Jewish martyrs at this time described in the books of Maccabees, two of which are in the Apocrypha. It is significant that this is the moment, when the Jews were suffering due to being faithful to God, that we see the first glimpses of the idea of judgment in the afterlife creeping into their belief system. I would also suggest to you that this is not coincidence (see the discussion of "Heaven and Hell" on pp. 182–83).

When hearing that the book of Daniel was not written during the same time period in which the story is set, some people conclude that there is an element of deception implied. But play along with the writer for a moment and pretend that the story *was* written during the time in which it is set, the Babylonian exile (mid-sixth or seventh century BCE). Then you can read the visions that Daniel has as if they are predicting events of the next few centuries—the kingdoms or empires that take over in succession—when in reality they have already happened. The message of hope here is that God has been with them all along, protecting the people and in control of all these things. It is implying that they can trust that God will continue to be with them in similar ways and that the reign of terror they are experiencing will soon come to an end.

We do the scriptures a disservice if we forget the writer's intended message of God's faithfulness and instead expect the book of Daniel to "play out" in our current situations today. If you read it closely, most of the symbols or creatures are interpreted within the book for you (2:31–45; 4:10–27; 7:2–27), and the references are all to groups of people living in or prior to the second century BCE (Daniel 11).

The Book of Revelation

The book of Revelation has some intensely gruesome images and symbolism. The fantastical description of how God will swoop in and destroy or judge all the enemies of his people makes up the majority of the book. But keep in mind it is not a literal prediction; it is a vision that is meant to encourage oppressed people and offer them a wisp of hope.

That said, as you read and think about Revelation, you might be intrigued to learn that Revelation almost wasn't included in the Bible. It was on a short list of books (along with Hebrews, 2 Peter, 2 and 3 John, and James) up for debate in terms of canonization. In the case of Revelation, some people did not think it had been written by someone associated with the early Jesus movement, and they were offended by the nature of the events it describes. Over the centuries, various people in the Church, including Martin Luther, have rejected the idea that Revelation was inspired by a loving God. Fascinating, eh?

Many people are not aware that the island of Patmos, which is where John reports to be when he wrote Revelation, was used as a labor camp of sorts, for political prisoners. What this means is that John had been arrested for political reasons, as he admits in Revelation 1:9, when he says that he is on the island of Patmos because of the word of God and the testimony of Jesus.

But why would the testimony of Jesus get people in trouble, politically speaking? Because, in worshiping only Christ, followers of Jesus Christ were not also giving the emperor his due. We have various moments in scripture and in non-canonical writings that attest to this being an important issue that followers of Jesus faced in the first and second centuries. The message to the church in Pergamum (Rev. 2:12–17) includes a reference to the "throne of Satan." Biblical scholars in the past thought this was a reference to the temple to Zeus from this town, and this temple is labeled accordingly in the museum in Berlin. But I think the wrong temple has been given this label. The overall language and symbolism in Revelation points to "Satan" being the emperor, and there was a large temple to the emperors in the center of the town of Pergamum. Zeus was not an issue for followers of Jesus; but showing honor to the emperors was a matter of life and death for them. Paying honor or reverence to the emperor, through something we refer to as the Imperial Cult, was expected of all citizens, regardless of religious beliefs. Participating in the Imperial Cult was simply a way of being patriotic, showing gratefulness for the security offered by the emperor. Followers of Christ who were not doing their share of honoring the emperor were thought to be ungrateful and most likely subversive. We know that some were arrested, told to pay homage to a statue of the emperor and to renounce Christ. If they did so, they would be let go. Some of the followers of Jesus who refused to do these things were executed.

It is worth considering that the letter of 1 Peter is also written to followers of Jesus who were suffering socially and politically because of their beliefs, but the author of 1 Peter takes a radically different approach to this suffering than what we see in Revelation. First Peter 2:17 tells people to honor the emperor above all else! The general message of Revelation is that the "emperor and his empire are going down!" First Peter was written by someone in prison in Rome, the capital of the empire, presumably for similar reasons that John was imprisoned on Patmos, far removed from Rome. The suggested response to the suffering in 1 Peter, however, is to do whatever it takes to stay alive. The "advice" in Revelation is to just hang tight and stay the course, for God is visiting soon.

This is, it seems to me, one of the most blatant examples of the Bible's human authorship. Two prisoners, arrested for the same reasons, giving advice to others in light of their experiences, and their messages could not be more different. Take a moment to think about this contradiction in light of beliefs about the Bible's inerrancy.

As you take the book of Revelation into your own hands, start with awareness of the book's unique and specific purpose. It is a vision or dream that narrates how God is going to give the Roman emperor, and all his trusty leaders, a gory death. All the symbolism in Revelation was referring to people or systems that were in place in the first century. The message of "hope" is that the torture and unjust suffering of the followers of Jesus, at the hands of their own political rulers, is going to end quite soon and will be turned on those who inflicted this suffering to begin with.

APOCALYPTIC SYMBOLS

Revelation's overall purpose is a lot more important than decoding the specific symbolism of the book's creatures and numbers. But those symbols are, nonetheless, the source of much fascination around this misunderstood piece of scripture and are central to the literary form John used to deliver this message. Some of the most curious symbols are the "four living creatures" and the lamb in Revelation 4–5. While I do not address these, specifically, it might interest you to compare those descriptions with some of the cartoon imagery we see in Monty Python movies. What I initially took to be unsettling and bizarre combinations of animals, humans, and angels in those movies I soon realized were taken from descriptions of creatures found in Ezekiel, Daniel, and Revelation!

144,000 (Revelation 7)

Who are these special 144,000 first mentioned in Revelation 7? Who knows? But instead of looking for literal people for this relatively small number to apply to, think of the symbolism it contains. The twelve tribes of Israel are all listed, which tells us that the people this was written to still identified with Judaism on some level. Then there is the symbolism of twelve in general. Each of the twelve tribes have 12,000 members among the servants of God. Taking a symbolic number, such as twelve or forty, and using a multiple of it was simply a way of intensifying the symbolism. In a sense, this number simply represents all the people, from among the descendants of Israel, who were faithful to their lives' end.

Washed in the Blood of the Lamb?

I used to sing several worship songs that drew on this idea. It gave me great comfort or assurance of being forgiven. Here it is, in Revelation: "They have washed their robes and made them white in the blood of the Lamb" (Rev. 7:14). This image of the blood of Christ as washing away one's sins is still being embraced today.

Have you ever stopped to think about what this image suggests? Blood, deep red blood, is thought to wash away people's impurities, which have built up due to their sins. And the now-purified state is symbolized by whiteness. The thing is, when something is washed, or drenched, in blood it will be far from white and "clean" as a result.

The idea of washing someone, or one's clothing as indicated in 7:14, in blood comes from the animal sacrificial system we discussed in chapters 5 and 10. The premise of the sacrificial system, you'll recall, was that taking a life was necessary for bringing God and humans back into a right relationship after humans have sinned. When an animal was killed for this purpose, the blood was often smeared all over the altar and sometimes sprinkled on the people. It's a gruesome picture but one we perpetuate when we sing hymns like "Are You Washed in the Blood?" and "Nothing but the Blood of Jesus."

What do you think about being "washed in the blood of the Lamb"?

"The Woman and the Dragon" (Revelation 12)

Two things stand out to me about this vignette: First, it is one of those moments in which the lack of chronology in this vision is rather obvious, further reminding us that the vision is symbolic and not predictive. Revelation 12:1–6 is talking about the mother of Jesus and her giving birth to him, which has obviously already taken place at the time that Revelation was written. It is included in the vision as a piece of the overall message of God's presence with the people.

Second is the reference to Satan or the Devil as a dragon. This is the one brief Newer Testament reference to "Satan" or "the Devil" having been thrown out of heaven. We get a much more developed version of this eviction of Satan from heaven in some apocryphal writings and in Milton's *Paradise Lost*, but not so much in the Bible. I encourage you to think about how influential this kind of language or imagery is, since it contributes to the now popular image of Satan as a discrete being, the personification of evil.

"The Beast" and "The Number of the Beast" (Revelation 13)

Ah, the beast. Here we are at last. The beast is described as having ten horns and seven heads (take a moment to try to picture that—the middle three heads have two horns, and the rest have only one). There are blasphemous names and all kinds of horrific things being said about this beast. The way this beast is also associated with the suffering of "the saints" suggests that the beast represents the emperors of the Roman Empire. The numbers seven and ten can be connected to the number of emperors. The symbolic message is that some of these emperors were attacked (see the reference to the "mortal wound" in v. 12) or were not as strong as others, but in ruling the known world, all the inhabitants of the earth bowed down to them. As part of the Imperial Cult, people were literally expected to bow down to figurines of the emperors. We also know that many of the titles given to Jesus Christ, such as "King of Kings," "Lord of Lords," "Savior," "Light of the World," "Son of God," and so on were ascribed to the emperors. Affirming a king other than and higher than the emperor was incredibly subversive.

The number of the beast is another popular symbol: 666. I have known people who would reject a license plate that has "666" in it or student IDs with three 6's in it (regardless of being next to each other or not). This number, on its own, holds some sort of meaning, doesn't it? How do you respond when you see this number?

It might interest you to know that some of the ancient manuscripts have an alternative number: 616. How could this be? Well, we get both numbers, 616 and 666, through a system of Hebrew numerology called *gematria*. This is a system in which every letter of the alphabet has a number associated with it. The sum of the numbers associated with a name is "the number" of that person. There were two different ways that people wrote the Emperor Nero's name: Caesar Nero or Caesar Neron. It just so happens that the number associated with "n" was 50, which gives us 666 for the longer version and 616 for the shorter version of his name.

Nero was one of the more vicious emperors of the first century when it came to the treatment of followers of Jesus. He liked to use them as tiki torches for his parties: cover them with tar and set them ablaze. He also started a fire in the run-down part of Rome and blamed it on the followers of Jesus. The destruction of those buildings just so happened to allow him to add on to his already large living quarters. Getting to blame it on a helpless group of people whose practices made them seem subversive to the empire was just a bonus. Nero's persecution of followers of Jesus, approximately 64–68 CE, is a fairly well-documented event, historically speaking.

There was another emperor in the mid-90s, Domitian, who was also quite vicious toward followers of Jesus. It is thought that Revelation was completed during Domitian's reign.

"The Lamb and the 144,000" (Revelation 14)

I find the description of the blameless 144,000, who had been redeemed, a bit disturbing. Notice why it is that they are said to be pure and blameless: they have neither "defiled themselves" (had sex) with women nor lied. Let me ask those of you who have had sex: Is that how you see the act of intercourse? Do you feel that you defile yourself every time you enjoy this natural aspect of human relations?

You also might want to notice that the author of Revelation was assuming that all these people were men, which does make populating the planet with them rather difficult. But that aside, what does it mean that these 144,000 male virgins are following the (male) Lamb, who is Jesus, wherever he goes? It is also worth noting that in 19:6–9, these same people are invited to the marriage supper of the Lamb. They represent the bride of Christ. So these 144,000 male virgins will symbolically "marry" Jesus, the Lamb of God? If you pause to consider these scenes, I think you can see why some scholars have suggested that this is a fairly homoerotic situation. Think I'm crazy for saying such a thing? Go read those passages for yourself and see what you think.

"Whore of Babylon" (Revelation 17)

Read for yourself the description of this "whore" found in Revelation 17:1–6.

There are four main things to consider from this segment of chapter 17. First, the "whore" is seated on many waters. These waters are interpreted later in verse 15 as many peoples and nations and languages. The Roman Empire included many different people groups. We know that the Greeks before them tried to create a unifying language, for instance, but the various groups of people would have remained.

Second, in verse 2 it says that the kings of the earth have committed fornication with this whore. Reading this politically, as makes sense given the context, this is a reference to the political alliances or international relations that took place at the time between Rome and other countries. This means that the "whore" is perhaps referring to the emperor himself, which is fascinating since this whore is described as being a female. (Do I sense some misogyny there, in personifying someone they hated as a female prostitute?) Regardless of who the specific person was thought to be, notice what is happening when the author applies the concept of *fornication* to international and political alliances. We see something similar in the Hebrew Bible, when the prophets refer to worshiping gods other than Yahweh as an act of adultery. I don't know about you, but I am rather sad that the biblical authors talk about sex in this way. The "ultimate sins" of people are time and again compared to "whoring around" or committing adultery. How might this use of sex as a metaphor affect peoples' beliefs about and attitudes toward sex?

Third, why "Babylon"? Consider the meaning of *Babylon* for the ancient Jews. Around the year 587 BCE, the Babylonians not only conquered Jerusalem and carried off thousands of Israelites into exile; they also destroyed the temple in Jerusalem, which was devastating to the identity, not to mention the morale, of the people. The Babylonians go down in history as horrific enemies of the Israelites. Thus we see, here in Revelation and in 1 Peter, a reference to Rome as "Babylon." The Roman Empire is the first-century version of the Babylonian Empire for the ancient Jews.

Finally, Revelation 17:6 says that the whore is drunk on the blood of the saints. This is a fairly clear nod to the literal suffering and executions of the followers of Jesus. This kind of comment, "the blood of the saints," occurs multiple times throughout Revelation.

"Fallen Babylon" (Revelation 18)

Notice that Revelation 18 opens with the claim that Babylon (Rome) has fallen. If you read through this chapter, you can see how its claims could be good news for those suffering terribly under Roman rule. Saying that Rome has fallen, even though it had not yet, would have been an expression of hope and confidence in God's provision. The fact that Rome did not "fall" in the next decade or so does not need to be upsetting; nor do we have to read Revelation as "not complete" until Rome did fall. Remember, this is a message of hope, not a literal prediction.

Verses 20–21 have a striking depiction of God's wrath judging Rome:

> Rejoice over [Babylon], O heaven, you saints and apostles and prophets! For God has given judgment for you against her.
> Then a mighty angel took up a stone like a great millstone and threw it into the sea, saying,
>
>> "With such violence Babylon the great city
>> will be thrown down,
>> and will be found no more."

It goes on to talk about the utter destruction of everyone in Rome, noting that artistic, musical, and regular everyday events would no longer take place there. Depending on your view of God, you might or might not really attribute this kind of devastation to God or God's wrath. But for those suffering at the time, one can see where the desire for this to be done to Rome and the Roman Empire's officials might come from.

You could say that this is what God's "righteous anger" at injustice looks like: God is legitimately wrathful because Jesus' followers are being mistreated. Perhaps. But what does it do that this kind of violent language and imagery is read by millions of people who cannot relate to the original recipients and their terrible situation? Even worse, what about when this language and worldview is taken up by the powerful in this world—the equivalent of the Romans or Babylonians today? Hmmm.

"Judgment Day" (Revelation 20)

Chapter 20 of Revelation refers to Satan, or the Devil, being thrown into a pit for one thousand years. This will be followed, according to this vision, with him being released for a time, finally to be thrown into a lake of fire and sulfur. There Satan, the beast, and the false prophet will be tormented, "day and night forever" (v. 10). The part of this

Heaven and Hell

Admittedly, there is no way that I can sufficiently describe what the Bible has to say about *heaven* and *hell*. So what I would like to offer here are just a few nuggets to get you thinking.

The first nugget is that in the earliest writings in the Bible we do not see any concept of a heaven, in terms of it being where our spirits or souls might go when our bodies stop functioning. The idea of an afterlife in the Hebrew Bible, initially, seems to consist primarily of our "souls" going to a place called "Sheol." (This is similar to what the ancient Greeks called "Hades.") It was a place, thought to be just under the surface of the earth, where our souls would go and simply chill.

The afterlife held neither the idea of eternal torture for living an evil life nor of eternal blessedness for being "righteous." At least, not at first.

This idea is so common to most of us today, so accustomed are we to the duality of heaven and hell, it is hard to fathom that the people who wrote most of the Hebrew Bible genuinely did not assume that our souls would suffer or rejoice for all eternity.

The first time we see this idea of being judged after we die sneaking into the thought and writings of Jews was when they began to be tortured and executed for their beliefs. A change in a belief is often set in motion by real-life experiences. For the ancient Jews, the idea ran something like this: Our God is all-powerful and just. Yet we are now suffering unjustly in this life specifically for being faithful. So it must be that God will "make things right" at some point. Since this kind of justice is not happening during this life, it must certainly be something that will happen after we die.

As this concept of the afterlife developed over time, it grew to include the idea of judgment after we die. Believing that God will punish their oppressors was a natural response to feeling helpless and was part of believing that God will ultimately "have their back." It seems, then, that the idea of "heaven" as a sanctuary for the righteous develops as a logical counter to the concept of hell. If "bad" people go one place, what happens to the "good" people? But notice, for instance, even in the book of Revelation, the 144,000 faithful do not take up residence "in heaven" but are starting a new thing on this planet. The holy city, the new Jerusalem, descends from the heavenly realm and settles on the earth (Rev. 21). The idea of everyone being sent "up into heaven" or "down into hell" on Judgment Day took time to develop as well.

There is an element of this idea of judgment that resonates with some people even today. It is somewhat understandable to want God to have the final word in judging people's actions. And, of course, there are biblical passages to back up this idea. But both apocalyptic messages and the belief in a Judgment Day are grounded in extremist worldviews and a desire for vengeance.

Some people suggest that without the idea of our sinfulness being judged after we die, we, as a human race, would be woefully evil and totally corrupt in our actions in this life. This argument is very similar to one of the justifications for the death penalty: that the threat of punishment is a deterrent to violent crime, even though, in the case of the death penalty, research tells us otherwise. Applying this thought to general human behavior suggests that humans are devoid of a moral compass and that only "the fear of God" will cause people to treat one another well. Take a moment to think about this assumption. What does it say about our potential for doing good? What does it say about our responsibility to make the world a better place? Does this reflect the way you think of humankind?

I can assure you that there are plenty of people who are deeply loving and kind, lacking in judgment of other people's actions, and seeking to make the world a better place, who do not rely on the idea of "heaven and hell" to motivate them. What does this say about the connection between religious beliefs and moral behavior?

passage directed to all people is found in 20:11–15. I hope you will read it before reading any further.

This is one of two places in the Newer Testament where we have the idea of a single Day of Judgment—where everyone who has died already and everyone still alive are judged for their actions on earth. I invite you to imagine the scene in verse 11 as if it were part of a movie. What kind of music would be playing in the background? What emotion would the people be projecting as they "fled from his presence," and found no place to hide? There is a reason that many people have been traumatized by this book. If the violent and gruesome scenes prior to this haven't upset you, the threat of this kind of a moment, when your life's actions will be judged by a terrifying and wrathful Judge, has the potential to evoke fear from the best of us. Doesn't it?

An eight-year-old friend of mine, Tessa Simone, has heard about this day, when those judged would be thrown into a lake of fire, presumably to burn there for all eternity. Her immediate response, without skipping a beat, was something along the lines of, "But that doesn't make any sense! You can't burn for eternity. Maybe for an hour or so, but you'd be burned up pretty quickly. That just doesn't make any sense." Ahh. Out of the mouths of children.

She makes a good point, doesn't she? What does it tell you about the person who wrote this kind of a scene, and who would wish this kind of a physical impossibility on his "enemies"? Have you considered what it does to children when we teach them to believe in such a fantastical method of torture?

"New Heaven and a New Earth" (Revelation 21–22)

So many of our contemporary movies and other depictions of apocalypses feature cataclysmic destruction of the planet. In Revelation, however, a new heaven and earth simply replace the current versions. For the author of Revelation, the climax of the story is in the judgment and destruction of the enemy. The end of the reign of terror is the message or the good news of Revelation, more like a movie's happy ending when the bad guys are defeated, the thunderstorm abates, and suddenly the sun comes out again and everything is at peace. All of our current associations of an apocalypse as the destruction of the planet, something we ought to prepare for or try to avoid, are a far cry from the initial message of apocalypses. Initially, it was good news! Initially, it was something that the recipients wanted to have happen, sooner rather than later. Initially, it was about the hope of an unjust world being replaced with a just one.

CONCLUSION

I have found, as I rack up the years on this planet, that I respond more passionately and wholeheartedly to an appeal to the good within me than to being shamed or told that I am sinful. There is a moment from my twenties that drove home this point well. A friend, after watching me at my wit's end trying to motivate a group of teenagers by yelling at them, suggested that honey attracts more flies than vinegar. He was spot on. Changing things around to a positive invitation to step up the pace made a world of difference, not only in the productivity of the people I was speaking to but also to the nature of the dynamic between us. A positive invitation appeals and sustains; anger and fear shut down the spark within us.

I would suggest that we take this same kind of an approach to the way we read or think about the book of Revelation. As with so many other passages in the Bible that can lead to harmful interactions between people or to hateful judgment to be passed over to others, we do not have to agree with the tactics employed here in Revelation.

Apocalypses are built on an assumption that the world's problems are too much for us, as humans, to address. But maybe the writers of apocalypses did not have it right. Perhaps we do not need to wait for God to intervene to right the world's wrongs. Maybe it is okay for us, collectively, to work together now to turn this world into a world of justice and peace.

 TAKE THE BIBLE INTO YOUR OWN HANDS

1. What have you understood the message of the book of Revelation to be in the past? Do you see any similarities in the meaning of apocalyptic writing for the original audience and the meaning many people of faith today find in it? Are these similarities justified?

2. Noting that Revelation's message is geared toward people in such extreme persecution and suffering that it seems that only God can fix the problem, what groups of people today do you think can relate to this message?

3. Do you find the idea of God pouring out wrath on earthly "enemies" comforting? Can you think of other ways to communicate the promise of God's protection to offer hope and encouragement for people?

4. How does learning that the ideas related to heaven and hell developed over time affect the way you think about those concepts? How might this influence the way you read about them in the Bible?

5. So many people think that the book of Revelation will "play out" in the future. How would you respond to them, given the historical and political realities that the author of Revelation was addressing in his own time?

12

Now What?

Some of you might be wondering, "Now what?" Questioning a literal reading of the Bible or the typical way of reading certain passages can set in motion even more questioning. I recall having quite a knee-jerk reaction to it all, thinking: "If this one thing about the Bible is not true, in the way I thought the whole Bible was true and trustworthy, then where does it stop? What is to keep someone from challenging all of it?" This is sometimes called the "slippery slope" issue.

I recall a sinking feeling in my own gut as I mulled over these issues initially. A change in something so central to a person's worldview can be deeply unsettling and disorienting. I can also recall seeing the look of anxiety on the faces of many people when they first allowed themselves to consider the implications of some of these facts. I imagine many of you had similar reactions at various points in this book. So I hope it helps to know that you are not alone. There are many people of faith who have confronted these issues in the Bible and come out the other side. Interestingly enough, they are often even stronger in their faith than when they began!

If those concerns apply to you, my intention is not to leave you in the lurch, with your entire faith system challenged. My ultimate intention has been to have you look at where you have placed your faith. Is it on the words in the Bible or on the God the Bible points to?

Or, for those of you who do not come with faith commitments related to the Bible, I hope that you also have a better sense of what the

Bible contains related to these topics. More than that, though, I hope that you can appreciate why people who hold these scriptures close are affected by them as deeply as they are. Perhaps this will allow you to have more informed conversations with others about the Bible.

Regardless of your reasons for reading this book, what I have intended to model for you is a critical thinking approach to scripture that respects it and the faith claims that people draw from it.

How has your view of scripture grown and changed as you have taken the Bible into your own hands? What sorts of things in scripture are you aware of now that you weren't before? I keep a list of insights students name after studying scripture this way for a semester. I've often heard reflections such as:

—A lot of people get raped.
—It doesn't specifically say that if you are gay you are going to hell.
—Nowhere does it say that if you have premarital sex that you go to hell.
—God is shown to have very human-like emotions.
—There's a lot of stuff preachers leave out.
—A lot of the books do not really help contribute to making the Bible holy.

While it's interesting to learn about the stories or aspects of scripture that often get overlooked, more important is developing your own way of reading and understanding the Bible. All the insights you have had as you read work together to create a lens for reading scripture in the future.

Personally, I hold my understanding of who God is and is not as my lens in every encounter with scripture. I have a litmus test for scripture and theological claims: If a biblical passage or theological doctrine endorses freedom, liberation, love, the fullness of life for all people, or a mature and responsible faith, then it is "of God." When I see a passage that depicts God as wrathful or as dealing death-blows to his supposed enemies, for instance, then that passage does not pass the test. When there are passages that contain belittling words or that endorse arbitrary restrictions of people, I assume those passages were inspired by human desires, not a loving and reconciling God. Most of all, I believe in the ability of human beings to make ethical, loving, and moral choices; this is what binds us together. I believe that when a biblical passage does not endorse such choices, then we need to be able to call it out instead of finding a way to uphold it anyway.

As I have talked through passages, I have held up my own lens for you to see how I view scripture. Your lens or litmus test will be your own, and perhaps it will be quite different from mine. The important part, for those of you who turn to the Bible for daily guidance or for theological claims, is to be aware that your engagement in the world is directly affected by how you read the Bible. I think it is important for you to be conscious of what your litmus test is and to be assured that it is okay if it is different from what you were taught it should be.

The Bible is not God. The Bible was intended to point us toward God. When it manages to do that, "blessed be!" When it does not . . . well, then you are allowed to say so and let it go. Permission granted.

44849673R10116

Made in the USA
Lexington, KY
10 September 2015